Feeding and Leading

By

RICHARD R. CAEMMERER

THE WITNESSING CHURCH SERIES

William J. Danker, Editor

CONCORDIA PUBLISHING HOUSE
ST. LOUIS, MISSOURI

Concordia Publishing House, Saint Louis 18, Missouri

Concordia Publishing House Ltd., London, W. C. 1

Copyright 1962 by Concordia Publishing House

Library of Congress Catalog Card No. 62-10385

Manufactured in the United States of America

Foreword

"An army travels on its stomach," said Napoleon — among other canny campaigners. A good officer looks first to the welfare of his men. Hungry, starving soldiers do not fight well.

It is particularly gratifying that the Concordia Series on the Witnessing Church can begin with the solid, sober Biblical facts of life presented by Dr. Caemmerer, head of Concordia Seminary's practical department and veteran professor of homiletics, as he demonstrates the inseparable connection between feeding and leading, between faith and witness, between church and mission. This man is so practical because he is so Biblical, so communicative because he is so theological.

Seldom have such demands been made on Christian people as today. It takes great inner resources for the individual just to get through the tensions and problems of each day. Around the globe in Europe, North America, in Asia, in Africa and Latin America, cultists and fringe sects are arising to supply the aching demand of people who find themselves desperately eager for spiritual strength and security. Seldom has the Christian church encountered such challenges as today. The polarization of power between East and West, the population explosion, the flaming tide of nationalism, and the renascence of non-Christian religions are some of the factors that place the Christian world mission in a totally new situation. With the recession of colonialism, the witness of the Christian church abroad no longer rests on political power. This is a great new fact of our era. In addition, racial barriers are crumbling, so that the white Christian no longer stands on an invisible pedestal as he confronts people of other races and cultures. No longer will other peoples tolerate the patronizing "downward slant." It infuriates them. We are dealing with political and cultural equals. Our witness cannot rest on gunboats or on nuclear bombs, but only on the power of the Spirit.

This is no day for the spiritual anaemia that has overtaken so much of Western Christianity. The activism of many American churches is like forced labor for concentration camp inmates fed on a starvation diet. It can end only in spiritual death. Ambitious programs in church building that now aggregate more than a billion dollars per year (spending $7 per year for brick and mortar for every $1 devoted to the world mission), enlarging church staffs and budgets, expanding home and overseas missions — these demanding tasks call for a high-protein diet for the workers. An elder in my first church used to say: "Don't whip

4

a willing horse." He would agree that it is even worse to beat a starving horse. Pastors and church workers must be experts in nutrition.

On the other hand, theology and Bible study are not an end in themselves. A high-fat diet in the U. S. A. coupled with insufficient exercise is carrying many to an untimely death. We have to work the calories off. The nourishment that is not expended in loving service and witness to others can cause spiritual bloating and blockage of circulation. To eat with no thought of others is to violate the fundamental law of the Kingdom — the law of self-giving. It is not easy to overcome mental laziness; it is not easy to study and to subject oneself to serious theological discipline. But it is easier to study than it is to love. Without self-giving love, theologians, pastors, and people don't grow, they just swell. The word for church in the Japanese language, "kyokai," means "teaching society." It can easily be misunderstood. Many people assume therefore that the church is a place where the ordinary person goes to learn. The church is, indeed, a teaching society, but one in which each and every member joins in the teaching, just as you don't join a glee club to be a listener but to be a singer.

To transform the church from a listening society to a witnessing society, powerful nutrition is needed. We need God acting now through the announcement of His mighty acts of redemption for His people. We need the Holy Spirit working through the Gospel of God's open-hearted love for creatures broken and torn from their Maker and from one another. People living in lavish outward material comfort and with

5

the internal aching hollowness of neurotic anxiety need to know that God loves them. Only so can they accept themselves and love other people. Pastors will have to become ever better cooks, setting an ever more lavish table. Every meal should be a Gospel feast, and the critical cases should have Biblical vitamin injections. Dr. Caemmerer sets a high standard here. He is a master chef. There is nothing niggardly about the way he sets his groaning board. Not content with dainty hors d'oeuvres — although they're on the menu, too — he slices huge steaks off the rump of the New Testament and serves them to his readers.

The idea, then, is that starving people now strengthened with the Gospel get up from the table, tie on their aprons, and begin cooking on the front burner, serving the Gospel to others. Here too many cooks don't spoil the broth. Every Christian is cooking for and feeding his fellow Christians. If they have been too weak to talk — let alone walk — before, now they can get the strength to put the Gospel into words. In a century that has often snidely deprecated the articulation of the Gospel, Dr. Caemmerer insists on its outspeech with all the power of the Word and the Spirit. But he is by no means content with a merely oral evangelism. This important emphasis of his entire book is so clear that he who runs may read.

People who are Gospel fed in "The Worshiping Church" will be at work feeding others in "Parish Nurture," in "Christian Giving," in "Community Witness," and in "World Outreach" — to list the headings of Dr. Caemmerer's richly nourishing chapters for the ministers of the church, both lay and clerical. After

6

all, the cooks have to eat well, too, and it isn't enough simply to snack and lick an occasional finger as they go along.

Leading and feeding go together — for sheep and for shepherd. This is at once a profound and practical New Testament truth. Readers will be as grateful to the author of this tasty, tested recipe as were the more than 125 pastors and other church workers attending the fourth annual Parish Administration Institute in 1960 conducted under the joint auspices of Concordia Seminary, St. Louis, Mo., and the Board for Missions in North and South America (an arm of The Lutheran Church — Missouri Synod). It was the unanimous desire of those present that these lectures should be made available to them and to others in published form.

We express our appreciation to all whose cooperation enables us to bring these lectures to a wider public, especially to Dr. Wm. Hillmer, executive secretary of the Board for Missions in North and South America, to Dr. Arthur C. Repp, academic dean of Concordia Seminary, and to Dr. O. A. Dorn of Concordia Publishing House.

It is our hope to present other provocative, relevant, and constructive discussions of the witnessing church in its many facets. We owe much in this area to a renascence of Biblical theology, and to a long-overdue reunion of theology and mission.

Laymen as well as pastors, missionaries, and other church workers and ministers — in the body of Christ in the Western as well as the non-Western world — will, we trust, welcome these planned presentations.

7

May they serve to build and nourish Christ's body for an ever richer, more winning witness to the multiplying millions of non-Christians in these days of exploding populations, fluid mobility, and rapid political and social change. May they remind us that the quality of the church's internal life, by which Christians lovingly serve and feed and build up one another, is in itself an important and effective witness to those without and in addition trains the members of the body for redemptive witness and loving service to the outsider.

WILLIAM J. DANKER

Contents

9

In the Worshiping Church

In these talks we are going to discuss the pastor as administrator. A flurry of discussion has arisen in the United States in recent years about the work of the pastor. Dr. Samuel Blizzard's studies have revealed that many pastors have a bad conscience about their pastorates because the work that they have been trained for (preaching and religious education and worship) takes up so small a portion of their energy; their major functions seem to be executive secretary, fund raiser, office manager, public relations consultant, and personnel director. Counseling has won status in recent years — but curiously as an imitation of the psychiatrist on a religious preserve rather than as a pastor. Conversely, H. Richard Niebuhr has coined a new term to define the complex of activities of the contemporary pastor: pastoral director.

The contribution of these pages will not swim against the stream of administrative assignments which the parish gives its pastor. For example, in churches

11

with a heritage of concern for religious education on the elementary level, the function of the pastor as a director of religious education has safe precedent. But I do want to attack the bad conscience which the pastor may have about administrative tasks. If they are worth doing at all, they are worth doing pastorally. Hence we want to discuss the theology of the pastorate; as we do so, we want to correlate with it a theology of the administrative labors of the pastor.

The five chapters of this contribution, we hope, can be understood cumulatively and not in isolation from each other. The initial subject puts a foundation under all the rest: The pastor is feeder and leader to the worshiping church.

I. THE PASTOR

Ephesians 4 gives a good working description of the pastorate. It relates the pastor to God as well as to the people. And it relates him not to people in general, but to the people of God in particular, to the holy Christian church. The church is made up of people who believe in Jesus Christ and who therefore are related to one another, wherever they are and wherever there is more than one of them. To that group and body of Christ in that place Jesus Christ has given gifts which Psalm 68:18 says Jesus has received from the Father:

Thou hast ascended on high, Thou hast led captivity captive; Thou hast received gifts for men; yea, for the rebellious also, that the Lord God might dwell among them.

12

These gifts are people, men of various sorts: apostles, prophets, evangelists, pastors and teachers. The apostles were the first ones sent out by Christ to speak His Gospel in every place. The prophets were the men and women in the early church endowed with special messages and abilities for telling this Gospel. The evangelists were uniquely the speakers of the message of the Gospel — some of them itinerant, some of them rooted to a single congregation. And then comes the label "pastors and teachers."

Pastor means shepherd. The shepherd leads his flock. The purpose of this leading is to remove it from danger, to bring it to safety, and to guide it over adequate and healthful forage. The shepherd feeds his flock; he sees to it that it has pasture and water. The New Testament, notably Acts 20:28, puts this double analogy of feeding and leading together, and always keeps it so: the leading is for the sake of feeding; the feeding implies the business of leading. Another term gets linked with pastor in this process: "Overseer" — ultimately translated "bishop," but originally meant to imply simply the double task of feeding and leading.

Eph. 4:11 brackets with "pastor" the term "teacher." "Teacher" suggests a process of staying with the flock so that it is nurtured, a technique of feeding by which the flock is helped to grow and achieve its goals. The New Testament concept of nurture turns toward the practical objectives of the Christian Gospel: the overcoming of fleshliness and irresponsibility within, and the unfolding of Christian love and responsibility in the callings of life toward the outside. Hence saying

13

that the pastor is simultaneously a teacher means that he undertakes a progressive and systematic routine of leading his people to increased efficiency in Christian faith and life.

These terms imply a program of labor on the part of the pastor and the people whom he serves by leading and feeding them. At the heart of this program is the fact that he shares with them what Ephesians 4 terms the "truth," a thing which can be spoken by one Christian to another; and what the parallel statement in Colossians 3 terms "the Word of Christ." The very spareness of these terms indicates the precision which underlies them. The "truth" is not merely a datum which Christ speaks but which He is, and it also denotes the plan of God brought to faithful fruition in Christ Jesus: to redeem mankind from its lost estate and bring it back under the kingdom of God and into one body under Jesus Christ. The Word of Christ is the message about His redeeming work on man's behalf, by which man is at peace with God and is put into one body with his fellow Christians under the headship of Christ. That the pastor feeds his people means that he brings the message of this redeeming work of Christ to bear on all aspects of their lives severally and mutually. That he leads them means that he brings them into the orbit of this Word and causes them to speak it to one another.

II. The Church

We have found it impossible, within just these few paragraphs, to speak about the pastor without speaking of the flock which he feeds and leads, the church to which he is a gift of the ascended Christ. In both the Ephesian and Colossian contexts which we have been discussing, the church is the body of Christ. That means that each member of the church is related to Christ as Head. Jesus Christ gave up His life for him, purchased him to belong to Him and serve Him. The church in any place, in the New Testament sense, is the believers in Christ, those who have been baptized into Him and who are nurtured by the Word of His redeeming work.

But these believers are also members to one another. 1 Corinthians 12 and Ephesians 4:13-16 describe the members of the church as functioning toward one another. Just as the members of the body play their role always for the sake of each other, so the members of the body of Christ function toward each other in conveying the life stream of Jesus' Word to each other. Thus the individual members are preserved from erosion by the world about them and the flesh inside of them. They are strengthened in their faith and for the output of life. They are built up — and here the picture of flock or of body gives way to the picture of a building — they are edified so that together, whether few or many, they become a strong building in that place which stands as a place where God is worshiped.

But the Christians in the place are never witnessing merely for themselves. Their witness reaches to their surrounding world right in the community where they live. The church is a building, but the individual Christian functions not merely in keeping his part of the building intact and playing his role as a living

15

stone in the building; he is ready to support the next layer of building stones: by love to receive the person outside of the body of Christ so that he, too, becomes one within the body of Christ. This happens as children are born into the Christian church and received by baptism, and as people who hear the Gospel of Christ are converted and share their lot with Christians.

In all of this the pastor as feeder and leader plays two roles. He preaches and teaches the Gospel of God, which converts to Christ and edifies men already in the body of Christ. He trains the Christians of the church to speak that Gospel so that they edify one another within the church and bear witness to their surrounding world so that its people give the Gospel a hearing. Thus the pastor simultaneously feeds and leads, trains and oversees the labors of those who are trained.

III. The Pastor and the Worshiping Church

Everything that we have said so far pertains to every chapter of our discussion. In the remainder of this section we focus on one function of the pastor within the church, and it is a major function of the pastor because it is a major function of the church, namely, that the church worships. In Ephesians 2:21 and in 1 Corinthians 3:16 the church is described as the temple of God. A temple is a place of worship. This picture comprises a number of facets. It means that the people who are a temple of God have God in their midst. It means that they are a visible assembly which indicates the presence of the invisible God among them, and they indicate His presence by their character and the honor which they pay to God. They are a temple of God as they safeguard His presence among them and ward off the unclean and profane.

To be the church at all, therefore, the church has to be the worshiping church, that is to say, the assembly of people who honor and adore God, who have Him present in their midst and safeguard His presence among them, and who bring Him the sacrifices of their selves, their praise, and their prayers. Also in their worship Christians act as members toward one another. They are priests toward one another, that is, they help each other sacrifice to God and they help to consecrate one another to God.

In all these phases of the worshiping church the pastor is to be leader and feeder. The "forage" is the Gospel of Jesus Christ. What is the leading? How is he teacher and nurturer? What is the administration that he exerts? Churchmen have often been more impressed with the crook with which the pastor hooks or pummels the sheep than with the food to which he leads them. The pastor leads as he feeds. Let us apply this principle to his administration of the worshiping church.

A. The pastor functions as an agent of the church through whom the Gospel initially beats on the ears of people and through whom they are baptized into the body of Christ and membership of the church. This is the rudimentary task of the pastorate, a leading and feeding in its simplest dimension, and therefore at first glance it is not involved with administration; the pastor is deploying himself into evangelistic

17

calls, counseling at desk and bedside, informal and professional conversations in his community, as well as the formal programs of membership forums and indoctrination courses for adults and catechetical courses for children and services of worship.

Actually however, the leading becomes at once most complicated and it enters upon administration in the exact sense of the term. The picture of the flock is incomplete, unless we would want to add the bellwether who lures the sheep into the paths the shepherd desires, or the herd which holds together in a pack against harm and straying. The pastor trains his people so that they can second or often precede his ministrations in the community, and this training and employing is an exacting program of administration (of which we shall speak more in the fourth unit of this series). But at this point we are concerned with stressing that the pastor's concern for his people, as they draw members of their community into the orbit of the church, is the concern that they be a worshiping community. Psychologically people always get only about as much as they are looking for. If they propose to join a church for the sake of its secular and social meaning — a parallel to Kiwanis or Soroptimists or American Legion — that is exactly what the church will have for them. If they propose to join the church as a program of psychiatry to be paid for only on the basis of voluntary contributions, that is what they will get. Incidentally, as soon as they discover that this is all they are getting, their loyalty to the church will give way to interest in other fraternities or tranquilizers. Hence a primary function in the pastor's administration of the

18

church is that he keep it visibly one of its kind in the world: an aggregate of people bound to God by faith in Jesus Christ and producing their service toward others in the name of God.

B. The operations leading his people to worship involve much more than that the pastor plan and officiate at services of worship. They comprise all of the operations which we shall consider in the second unit of this course as we discuss parish nurture; for everything that the pastor does so that his people grow in faith and spiritual life contributes to their worship of God and awareness of His primacy in their lives. At this point it must be said that the contributions to the worship life of the church by all of the religious education and group work in the congregation are not automatic. For religious education can mean merely the business of teaching others, or of learning Biblical facts, and may overlook growth in awe of the most high God and growth in the practice of proclaiming His grace. And group work may merely satisfy the interests of people in one another and give a bit of antiseptic recreation for which religious labels and devotional practices are merely a front. Hence if the educational and social activities of the church are genuinely to contribute to the worship of its members and the witness of the church as a witnessing community, they must include deliberately planned and explicit elements of worship and of training for worship.

Already several courses of adult instruction for church membership revolve about the church's worship, the understanding of its worship forms, the practical use of the means of grace, and the accepting of responsibility for the brother in the services and occasions for worship. All this is most useful. But it is important that those who are already church members also have the meaning and the practice of worship refreshed in their own consciousness. For the great bane of the church is the absentmindedness, not to say the absenteeism, of its members at worship. Forms suffer from thoughtless mouthing. Hymns are sung because people enjoy singing. The officiating of the pastor, whether in a full-fledged liturgical service or in a simple devotional, is regarded as a sign that it is a religious occasion rather than a structure in which the member of the church is sharing. Hence frequent alerting to the meaning and process of worship is necessary in group activities, by means of special study institutes, in Bible classes, and in programs of home study and worship. At the heart of all of these programs there must be not merely talking about worship, but worship itself.

This brings us to the major task of the pastor in administrating a worshiping church: his conduct of its formal worship. Traditionally practical theology differentiates between parish administration, and liturgics or the conduct of the worship service. Actually the two are so close that they overlap. For the pastor has to lead his people to worship as a shepherd leads his sheep to pasture. This means that the leading has to be effective and the occasion of worship has to be genuine pasturing.

The leading to worship has to be effective. The admonitions to come to church and the complaints against the absentees are often so trite that people listen to them without hearing. Actually the pastor must practice much more than admonition and complaint. The service of worship must be a thing which the worshiper understands; he must be trained to appreciate every item of it — on pain of committing the sin of blasphemy if he doesn't, and the pastor compounding the felony. Perennially the church hears a wave of counsel to simplify or colloquialize its worship forms. This is one answer to the pastor's concern that he properly lead and feed; but by the third time the new version is used the same lags of inattention and staleness might be apparent. Rather must the entire fabric of the church's life be woven about the endeavor to have people worship consciously and understandingly. As the member of the church looks forward to a service of worship in which he worships and knows what he is doing, he will want to come, and the first great task of leading will be achieved. That means that the member must think of each service as an opportunity: for praising the God who is good to him and on whom he depends for every moment of his life, for praying to that God in concert with his fellow members, for strengthening his own hold on that God through the repeated assurances of God's mercy, and for sharing in mutual strengthening by the interchange of Gospel in hymn, sacrament, sermon, and worship responses.

Church administration reaches its peak as the pastor constructs a worshiping company which encourages to common attendance. This begins in the family, and the pastor has to train for parental admonition that is not just giving orders, but the kind that holds up opportunities for worship and the intake of life from God. It moves on through the customs and habits of the congregation. The pastor has to run a tight ship. Ushers, organist, and choir have to look as much concerned in common worship as the people are supposed to be. The pastor must seem as manifestly eager and joyous at the praise of God and the intake of Word and Sacrament as he wants the people to be. The facilities for worship — whether a cross on a hillock at a picnic vesper or the full apparatus of a church building with art and paraments, music and hymnody, ventilation and maintenance — must glow with the marks of painstaking preparation. Saint Peter said that the great impulse for wanting the sincere milk of the Word had to be that the babe had tasted and found it good; and the pastor is responsible for making each service of worship so memorable that each subsequent one is anticipated with eagerness.

The pastor has to train the church to know and feel what worship is, we have been saying. The Christian's worship is a complex thing because on the one hand it is the response of the Christian to what God has already made him, God's own man in Christ; and on the other hand it is an occasion at which the Christian grows in that membership under God in Christ and becomes better enabled to respond. This is another way of saying that worship is simultaneously sacramental and sacrificial. The pastor is responsible for leading and feeding in both of these areas.

The word "worship" denotes primarily the sacrificial. Hence the pastor trains his people to bring their sacrifices of themselves, of one another, and of the tokens of their self-giving. They do this in their entire lives, which are a reasonable service. But they do this outstandingly in the activities in which they join together and stimulate one another to this end. Central it is that they speak their thanks and praise to God. They think of Him as high and good, and they tell Him and one another and everybody who will listen. In so doing they reflect upon His goodness toward them as it actually obtains. Hence every act of worship, no matter how formal or populous, is an intensely personal thing; the worshipers are thinking about their own God at work in their own lives. But this means that the entire pastorate must revolve about the leading of people to bring their sacrifice of praise, and the common worship of their total number is the climax. A congregation of Christians should be characterized not just by senseless activism, or torpid lethargy, or dogged sense of duty, or institutional lockstep, but by the spirit of praise to God which permeates the entire group and infects the world round about. This takes not merely things to praise God about — they are obvious — but it takes routines of speaking the praise, and of cultivating the spirit to sing the praise with a will.

A final element in the training for worship involves leading the members of the church to seek the sacramental. That is a gift from God; but it is a gift that God gives through means and through agents. He gives it through the means by which His redeeming act in Christ is brought into the memory and the mood. These are the message of the Gospel in lessons, responses, hymns, addresses, and the sacraments. These attach God's redemptive act in Christ to the signs He has ordained: water in Baptism, and Christ's own body and blood by means of bread and wine in Holy Communion. But God proposes to give this to His people through the agency of His people. Every worshiper thus becomes a person not only receiving God's grace through the means, but sharing it from one to another. St. Paul says that Holy Communion is a bread and a cup which Christians share with each other, and thus they share Christ's body and blood (1 Corinthians 10:16); and the writer to the Hebrews says that as Christians tell each other about the High Priest through whom they have access to God, they cause each other to grow in love and good works. (Hebrews 10:19-25)

C. This leads us to the climax of the pastor's work in leading and feeding the worshiping congregation: his actual administration of the service of worship. Everything we say here applies to the simplest and the most complicated; the extemporaneous word and song at twilight in a youth vesper and the most ornate festival Communion. So far we have been saying that the pastor as shepherd must lead his people to the pasture; now we are saying that when they are there, he has to see to it that they eat. Bantering words are said in many a lay home about being able to lead father to sit in a pew, but you can't make him listen. Suppose he does listen? What does he hear?

Actually almost everything that should be said on this subject is set forth in St. Paul's chapters in First Corinthians 10 to 15, and said to exactly this point. The Corinthians suffered from a deterioration of worship. Holy Communion had become the occasion of class conflict and drunkenness. Worship services had degenerated into the parading of hysterias by men and women claiming to be filled with the Spirit. These chapters are not so much a doctrinal handbook on the gifts of the Spirit or a treatise on worship as they are a piece on pastoral administration, where the apostle-pastor is trying to get the people to pasture on God's Word of life and share it with one another when they gather for worship and the Sacrament.

Two elements are interwoven in these chapters. The one brings this entire section under the subject of administration; it shows St. Paul busy as an over-seer of his people. This is the element which prizes the functioning of the Christian in the church as a member within the body of Christ for the sake of every other member. St. Paul is not so much concerned that he or other professionals be regarded as splendid technicians, or that certain unusually gifted Christians be given headship among the rest, but he is concerned that the gift of the Holy Spirit which every Christian has be put to work for the good of the entire group. The particular gifts or tasks which he describes Christians as possessing are all useful for the one common aim of edifying, building up, all the rest. Some of them we shall discuss under the topic of nurture. But most of them fit already at this point under the subject of common worship. For here are the people who have insight into the meaning of God's Word of grace. Here are people ready to speak their faith in Christ to one another. Here are others who can put the right estimate on teaching. Here are people gifted with the utterance essential for praising God. Here are Christians who can guide and lead others in their common tasks and others who can do the steady and basic chores that are necessary for the whole. All of them exist for the sake of edifying the entire body. Whether the given element of worship be sacrificial or sacramental, the gifted Christian at that moment, as he shares in it, can make an essential contribution to the spiritual health of others. He wills to do so, for he loves his brother.

The other element primary in these chapters concerns that which is truly edifying in common worship. Not everything will do. Whatever can't be understood is ruled out. Whatever makes suspicious and diverts the minds of the worshipers from the main track must simply be given up. "God is not the author of confusion, but of peace" (1 Corinthians 14:33). St. Paul is trying to help his readers practice the edifying thing, and so he gives them a sample: his own practice.

> I declare unto you the Gospel which I preached unto you, which also ye have received and wherein ye stand, by which also ye are saved, if ye keep in memory what I preached unto you; unless ye have believed in vain. For I delivered unto you first of all that which I also received: how that Christ died for our sins according to the Scriptures, and that He was buried, and that He rose again the third day according to the Scriptures. (1 Corinthians 15:1-4)

St. Paul digresses to confute the disbelief in the resurrection which might greet his words; then he comes back to the main track, the exhortation to worship together – with the Gospel of Christ as primary shared message of power by which the total church is edified:

> Therefore, my beloved brethren, be ye steadfast, unmovable, always abounding in the work of the Lord, forasmuch as ye know that your labor is not in vain in the Lord. (1 Corinthians 15:58)

The liturgical forms of the church, ingrained in centuries of mutual edification, are useful devices for keeping this Gospel pasturage paramount in worship. Holy Communion is a means by which the individual not merely receives the assurance of the forgiveness of sins for himself, but becomes a promoter and sharer of it with his fellow members: "As often as ye eat this bread and drink this cup, ye do show forth the Lord's death till He come" (1 Corinthians 11:26). Preaching has undergone much distortion through the years; some comes out like the shouting of a would-be Amos over the sins of communists and others safely absent from earshot; or it seeks merely to summon to conversion as though the people present were all heathen; or it parades an apparatus of quotations from authors ancient and modern and a profusion of techniques for making people comfortable. But if the pastor feeds and leads and he, as is usual, is the preacher, then let him feed with that sermon and preach Jesus Christ and Him crucified, which is the one message that builds faith and the one message that stirs to improved life. Furthermore that is the message for which a Christian congregation called him as preacher – if it knew what it was doing. For the people in the pew are preaching that message, they have called the preacher to speak it on their behalf; he is a servant of the people as well as of God. And the preacher's administration of the worshiping congregation involves helping it want to speak and to reinforce the message which he speaks, and helping it want that message to be the glad news of the grace of God in Christ Jesus applied to the immediate and personal problems, great and small, of the people present.

The services in which the pastor is directly an officiant are, of course, a primary avenue of feeding and leading. But he is responsible for all the others which his people conduct: the simple prayers of mother and child, the family altars, the family sessions with the hymnal around the piano, the devotionals in the church organizations which are led by members. Here he practices oversight, not simply as a censor, or as a distributor of the proper prayerbooks and formularies, but as a man concerned whether his people worship God together at all outside of the brief hour on Sunday mornings. He will have programs of personally visiting every family in his congregation and leading in their household devotions. He will organize every-member-visitation projects not for the sake of raising cash but for getting fellow Christians into each other's homes to pray with one another about the welfare of each other and their church and its tasks and for their entire world and its call for witness.

The reason why many pastors find seemingly secular or neutral tasks preempting their abilities while the theological and Biblical ones seem to shrivel in extent is not, basically, lack of faith or even people's unspirituality. It often begins with the situation that the pastor is not as resourceful, imaginative, busy in devising the routines of leading to the Gospel of life as he is in fund raising or the manipulations of group work. In part this is due to a false optimism. He imagines that if he says prayers at group meetings and prepares sermons faithfully and has the church ready at the stated hours on Sundays for worship, this is just about what it takes; this automatically pumps the sacred forage into the bellies of the sheep. In part it is a shyness to confront sacred things and to raise the important questions. What if our Lord had been shy with Martha, who was busy and troubled about feeding her noble Guest for the life that perishes, but had no imagination for the food for the life that does not perish and which is the better part? Nor was our Lord shy about pointing out the folly of the man who had good crops and built bigger barns but was not rich toward God.

The pastor is the one specialist in the community, and in the experience of his people, who is concerned professionally for the one thing needful on behalf of every one of them. Let the pastor himself grow in the resourcefulness with which he alerts to the meaning of eternal life and with which he deploys the spiritual gifts of all his people so that he constructs a congregation that is a community of people rich toward God, visibly strong in praise and adoration.

In Parish Nurture

In St. Paul's great list of parish helpers in Ephesians 4:11, he brackets the title "pastor" with its equivalent, "teacher." That word tends to bring administrative tasks to mind: appointing monitors, playing a part in institutional schedules, purveying teaching materials and sensory aids, and working with and under a staff. But we are bracketing the term with "pastor," and we are viewing it in a context of New Testament theology. Here that term always shares in the concept of nurture. That the pastor is a teacher means that he is responsible for the nurture of the church in which he functions. He is responsible for that nurture by feeding the people who are to grow in grace and faith and by equipping the people among whom he works to nurture one another.

I. The Structure of Nurture

Also in secular contexts we say that the teacher nurtures. He contributes to intellectual skills, he supervises physical maturation, and is concerned for improved relation of his pupil with his world and his fellow pupils. As we view the pastor in his administration of the church, we realize that he shares all of these concerns particularly in the dimension of man's life toward God. He aims at the growth of people — "grow in grace and in the knowledge of our Lord and Savior Jesus Christ" (2 Peter 3:18). He aims at growth — not merely of the people of the church individually — but of all: that they might all together grow up into the one smoothly functioning organism which we call the local church (Ephesians 4:12-16). See the picture in the Phillips version:

His gifts were made that Christians might be properly equipped for their service, that the whole Body might be built up until the time comes when, in the unity of common faith and common knowledge of the Son of God we arrive at real maturity — that measure of development which is meant by "the fulness of Christ." We are not meant to remain as children at the mercy of every chance wind of teaching and the jockeying of men who are expert in the crafty presentation of lies. But we are meant to hold firmly to the truth in love, and to grow up in every way into Christ, the Head. For it is from the Head that the whole Body, as a harmonious structure knit together by the joints with which it is provided, grows by the proper functioning of individual parts to its full maturity in love.

The growth for which the pastor nurtures and supervises nurture is therefore the growth of people,

31

individually and mutually, in Christ and under God. Note that the New Testament forces us to view simultaneously the growth and the means by which the growth is nurtured: the growth for which the pastor is responsible as he feeds and leads his people, and the pasturage with which he feeds to produce the growth. This food for growth, and therefore the heart of the administration of the nurture of the church, is the Gospel of Jesus Christ. Ephesians 4:15 calls it the truth.

This entire subject will come into clearer focus if we spend a few moments in discerning what we mean by the truth. In secular education we respect the truth, we train to seek it and to appreciate it. We mean by it everything that is true, exact, correct in the terms of its own norms. We are not dealing here with such an abstraction. When Jesus said (John 14:6) that He is the truth, or when He called the Holy Spirit the Spirit of truth (John 14:17), He did not refer to any complex or abstraction of human knowledge; the Spirit, He says, is He "whom the world cannot receive, because it seeth Him not, neither knoweth Him." But Jesus was speaking of a truth that has to do with God. Before He ever made the world, God proposed to redeem it from sin and death by His own Son Jesus Christ. He announced that plan through the ages of the Old Testament. And when the time was right, He made His promise come true in Jesus Christ, and the event came to pass for which the Psalmist prayed:

Show us thy mercy, O Lord, and grant us Thy
salvation.

> I will hear what God the Lord will speak, for He
> will speak peace unto His people and to His
> saints. . . .
> Surely His salvation is nigh them that fear Him,
> that glory may dwell in our land.
> Mercy and truth are met together; righteousness
> and peace have kissed each other.
> Truth shall spring out of the earth; and
> righteousness shall look down from heaven.
> (Psalm 85:7-11)

Ephesians 4:15 puts "speaking the truth" into one word, which we might translate "truthing" (var. "doing the truth"), namely, that Christians are to bring God's plan of redemption in Jesus Christ to come true in one another. "Speaking" is an apt phrase for it because at the heart of the program of Christian nurture is talk: talking about Jesus Christ and His redeeming work to one another, "holding forth the Word of life," as St. Paul puts it to the Philippians (2:16). The church which is functioning as the body of Christ is therefore composed of people who speak the truth to one another, make the truth effective in one another, in love, says Ephesians 4:15; or in the language of Colossians 3:15, 16, it is a company of Christians who are governed by the peace of God in their hearts, and so they cause the Word of Christ to dwell in them richly in all wisdom, "teaching and admonishing one another in psalms and hymns and spiritual songs. . . ."

We still are not seeing clearly, however, if we are thinking of print on a page or lessons to be learned out of a book. The truth is God's plan coming true.

His plan is not just that small boys or old grandfathers are able to recite words, or definitions of religious concepts. His plan is that the small boys and their grandfathers and the whole church of God be people in whom He, God, is Himself at work and alive. Learning words and definitions helps in the process, but that is only a help. The Bible is a means toward that end but always only a means. The great objective of Christian nurture is that people belong to God, that He and His Spirit and His Son are enthroned as rulers in their hearts, and that these people therefore carry out the purposes for which God has placed them in the world and recaptured them from sin and the devil to fulfill His purposes. The truth is the account of the recapture; it is the telling of a military campaign, not as ancient history, but as a proclamation that sets the person free from death and the devil as he listens to it, and re-enlists him in the army of God. To use another picture: the truth is not an article in a magazine about a family, but it is a parent instituting suit to adopt a child, and telling the truth is causing this child to find his place in the family of God again.

This speaking of the truth is therefore the heart of Christian nurture. Probably the most dramatic picture of growth in the New Testament is in the Epistle to Titus. This young man had been sent to the island of Crete, which had a materialistic civilization suspiciously like our own, in order to set up a firmer organization of the Christian church in that place. There were Christians throughout the island, some of them veteran in their membership in the church; and he was to go and initiate the preaching that would cause them to produce the good works for which God begets and nurtures His children. He was embarrassed about it, for he was probably younger than many of the people to whom he was to bring the message and he was aware of his own shortcomings and immaturity. St. Paul then gives him the splendid prescription for building the mature and fruitful church which becomes stereotyped in the festivity of Christmas and the memory tasks of the Catechism (Titus 2:11–3:8 RSV):

> For the grace of God has appeared for the salvation of all men, training us, so that we renounce irreligion and worldly passions, and to live sober, upright, and godly lives in this world, awaiting our blessed hope, the appearing of the glory of our great God and Savior Jesus Christ, who gave Himself for us to redeem us from all iniquity and to purify for Himself a people of His own who are zealous for good deeds. Declare these things; exhort and reprove with all authority. Let no one disregard you. Remind them to be submissive to rulers and authorities, to be obedient, to be ready for any honest work, to speak evil of no one, to avoid quarreling, to be gentle, and to show perfect courtesy toward all men. For we ourselves were once foolish, disobedient, led astray, slaves to various passions and pleasures, passing our days in malice and envy, hated by men and hating one another; but when the goodness and loving kindness of God our Savior appeared, He saved us, not because of deeds done by us in righteousness, but

in virtue of His own mercy, by the washing of regeneration and renewal in the Holy Spirit, which He poured out upon us richly through Jesus Christ our Savior, so that we might be justified by His grace and become heirs in hope of eternal life. The saying is sure. I desire you to insist on these things, so that those who have believed in God may be careful to apply themselves to good deeds.

From this notable excerpt and its parallels we are ready to build the structure of Christian nurture. It begins and it is sustained by the proclaiming of an event that has already occurred, the redeeming work of Jesus Christ, who was born into the world, lived and died and rose again, in order to restore men to God and give His life back into their hearts. This redeeming work and the Word of it saves people, rescues them from the death and doom that is man's lot in his rebellion against God. But this redeeming Word at the same time applies to people who have come to faith so that they might produce the fruits of their restored relation with God, the fruits of character and service among men. We are apt to think of "Christian nurture" as a process by which people, young or old, who before were poorly informed in the teachings of the Christian religion now become acquainted with them and occasionally have their memories refreshed about them. But Christian nurture and training in the terms of the New Testament is at once more simple and more comprehensive. It is more simple in that it always applies one great fact to the individual, no matter how well he knows it or how recently he has been told, namely, that God has restored him to life and peace through the redeeming work of Jesus Christ. It is more comprehensive in that nurture, in the Christian sense, always produces results from this fact and the Word of this fact; our Lord said that the kingdom of God and God's own rule in a man always was the business of producing a yield like the ear in a shaft of wheat (Matthew 13). This fruit is raised in all situations of life. It involves cramping and pinching off the inner bent to evil and irresponsibility which is the fruit of the rule of Satan in the heart, and it involves developing the individual so that he invests more and more of himself in service to his fellowmen and particularly in the increasing of the spiritual life of his fellow Christians.

The pastor in person feeds his people with this truth, seeks to make God's plan come true in them by proclaiming God's great work for them in Jesus Christ, and endeavors to apply that Word to them for the sake of producing the particular fruits of the Christian faith and life in practical situations. When we say that, we say that the pastor as feeder is playing the role of preacher or guide of worship or educator or evangelist. He is laboring to nurture his people and to administer the Word of life to them. But what is his work when he administrates parish nurture?

This is the bearing of the magnificent verse in Ephesians 4 which has been disfigured in the minds of so many Christians because of several commas.

He gave . . . pastors and teachers: for the perfecting of the saints, for the work of the ministry, for the edifying of the body of Christ; till we

37

all come in the unity of the faith and of the knowledge of the Son of God, unto a perfect man, unto the measure of the stature of the fulness of Christ. (Vv. 11-13)

This has usually been understood to mean: God gave pastors to make saints perfect; pastors are to do the work of the ministry; pastors are to edify the body of Christ until each member of it is strong in the faith and is a perfect man. But take out the commas! He gave pastors and teachers for perfecting the saints for the work of the ministry which the saints are to do! The saints are the ministers, the servants! Their service is that they edify, build up, the body of Christ. They lead one another into an ever stronger unity of the faith and of the knowledge of the Son of God. As they do so, they produce in the church, out of the many different people who belong to it, one perfect man, whose shape and pattern is that of Christ Himself, who is the Head of the church and fills out each individual so that all together become fitted perfectly into the pattern of the mutually helpful company.

Ministry, in this sense, is the work of every Christian. The pastor as feeder and leader, then, is in the business of "perfecting" the saints. The word is also used of the ship's chandler, who fitted out the ship at the dock with sails and rigging, water and stores, and perhaps even a crew, so that it would be ready to make its voyage.

A congregation of Christians is a kaleidoscopic group, whether it be 10 or 2,000. It is the church when individuals sit and listen, when they answer questions or share in the forms of worship, and especially when each one of them is by love serving each other one. The pastor is there to equip the individual member of the church to render this service to others. The tool at his disposal — just as it is the tool at the disposal of the members for their mutual ministry — is the truth, speaking the truth in love. This is administration in its most literal meaning, this is "oversight" or "the work of a bishop": the pastor becomes the energizer and guide of his people so that as many as possible of them, and each one of them as richly as possible, play their role in nurturing their fellow Christians. Parish nurture isn't just the end product of the Christian who is at the end of that chain reaction. But nurture is a good term to apply to the individual who is performing that building and edifying service.

II. The Modes of Structuring the Nurture

We have seen, in most general terms, the structure of Christian nurture for which the pastor is the responsible administrator. Let us investigate more closely the detail of this process. The epistles in the New Testament give a good picture; for the apostles themselves are serving in an administrative capacity as they write, and they are setting up the details of the nurture in actual operation.

As we confront these details we are impressed on every turn with the fact that the leading, the oversight, and the directing of human beings in their tasks toward others is always simultaneously feeding. There are two broad structures for nurture which work simultaneously in the Christian church: the gifts of the Spirit, and the Christian callings. The pastor is to be a chief director and deployer of these gifts of the Spirit; he is to be a trainer for carrying out the purpose of the Christian at work in his calling.

The primary document on the gifts of the Spirit is 1 Corinthians 12. At our first contact with this chapter we are struck with the fact that the gifts are not described so much as "talents" or "abilities" which the Holy Ghost takes over in the increase of the Christian life in the person. There are such processes, doubtlessly; 1 Peter 4:10, 11 counsels Christians to utilize the Spirit so that their every word and act of service may be empowered by Him, and this seems to be the lesson which our Lord is teaching in the parables of the talents and the pounds (Matthew 25; Luke 19). But in 1 Corinthians 12 the gifts of the Spirit have to do with the tasks of edifying the church and the working of men within the church for the common good:

> There are diversities of gifts, but the same Spirit; and there are differences of administrations, but the same Lord. And there are diversities of operations, but it is the same God which worketh all in all (5, 6). To each is given the manifestation of the Spirit for the common good. (V. 7 RSV)

This means that the use of the gifts of the Spirit is simultaneously pastoral and administrative; all of them have to do with Christian nurture, with building the faith and life of church people.

The apostle describes some of these operations at work. Here a man has the ability to produce a godly course of action in men, "the word of wisdom"; another has the ability to draw men into the experience of God

40

at work in their midst, "the word of knowledge"; another has the gift of supreme trust in God under adversity; another the power of healing by the Spirit; another the achieving of the fruits of the Christian faith that are a demonstration to the unbelieving world; another can speak the Christian religion well; another has skill in exploring the intentions and the truthfulness of religious teachers; another can speak with eloquence; and another can interpret the eloquence of the Scriptures and of other Christians.

The purpose of all of this array of ability and Christian service going on in the church is not that some are recognized as being more highly favored than others, for all have a gift in one respect or another; it is not the Christian way to rate one gift of the Spirit above another. But the purpose of them all is always that "the members should have the same care for another."

> Whether one member suffer, all the members suffer with it; or one member be honored, all the members rejoice with it. Now ye are the body of Christ, and members in particular. (Vv. 25-27)

This is our point: The pastor labors in the midst of the group to maintain the service and helpfulness of each toward all. St. Paul lists the people who were helpful in deploying these gifts: apostles, prophets, teachers; he enumerates the gifts: miracles, healings, helps, governments, and tongues. He writes this letter so that the people of Corinth might be led to exert the gift which they all had in common, namely, Christian love, for the good of all; and so that they might accept his suggestions for administrating their gifts. Interesting is the brace of gifts which he singles out, "helps, governments," special tasks of helpful service, and leaders ("administrators," RSV). Again the church has dallied through the ages with the vision of the pastor with the hooked staff, and very early the distortion arose in the church of putting the clergy in echelons of power over one another, mimicking the ranks of authority in secular government. To the present moment you can find learned treatises exploring the so-called authority of the pastorate or of administrative functionaries placed by church denominations over other pastors. But Jesus said:

> Ye know that the princes of the Gentiles exercise dominion over them, and they that are great exercise authority upon them. But it shall not be so among you; but whosoever will be great among you, let him be your servant; and whosoever will be chief among you, let him be your slave; even as the Son of man came not to be ministered unto, but to serve, and to give up His life a ransom for many. (Matthew 20:28 AV, altered)

And St. Peter echoes it:

> Feed the flock of God which is among you, taking the oversight thereof, not by constraint, but willingly; not for filthy lucre, but of a ready mind; neither as being lords over God's heritage, but being examples to the flock. And when the Chief Shepherd [Pastor] shall appear, ye shall receive a crown of glory that fadeth not away. (1 Peter 5:2-4)

42

The "governments" which St. Paul describes in 1 Corinthians 12:28 are termed, interestingly enough, not by some secular title, but *kyberneseis*, which means helmsmen. The steersman of a sailing vessel was a man of distinction all right, and the progress of the vessel depended on his skill and devotion. But he had no power whatsoever; the ship moved only as the wind filled its sails, and his purpose was to point the ship at such an angle that the wind was constant and the progress of the ship unhampered. In this great chapter on the gifts of the heavenly *pneuma* we find it irresistible to believe that the apostle is thinking of the director of church work as a person who serves his purpose only as he keeps the wind of God, the Holy Ghost, blowing into the spiritual life and heart of the people to the end that they arrive at their destination and fulfill the purpose for which God puts them together in the church. The Spirit of God, however, functions only as He speaks in the hearts of men of Jesus, and keeps repeating there what Jesus Himself held before them concerning His redeeming work; the pastor gets his people to hear and speak that Word.

The other great array of teaching in the New Testament on the functioning of nurture in the Christian church concerns the Christian callings. God's people are His because He has called them by the Gospel and made clear to them that they belong to Him, for they have been purchased by the blood of Jesus Christ (2 Timothy 1:9-12). The pastor and preacher functions in reminding men of God of this fact, keeping this call coming in their lives. But the called people are themselves put into the situation that they

43

speak forth this call; the apostle urges Christians to "stay in their callings," namely, in whatever station of life they find themselves, to keep active in speaking this great call with which God has called them (1 Corinthians 7:13-24; cf. Ephesians 4–6 and 1 Peter 2–4). We shall later consider the pastor's task in administrating the community witness of his parish. At this point we say a word about the functioning of the calling in parish nurture — first of all in the spiritual life and growth of the Christians themselves.

Here the New Testament conveys its most urgent teaching concerning the pastor's function in preserving the unity of the parish. The spiritual growth and nurture of the congregation depends on the connection between Christians, their will to speak to one another and to forgive each other's frailties even as they recognize them and seek to remedy them. Conversely, where the Christian congregation falls into contention and dissension, where the lines of communication between Christians fail, the spiritual vitality of the church declines and it becomes a laughingstock before the non-Christian community. St. Paul says that the person who does not discern the Lord's body, that is to say, put the supreme estimate on the worth and importance of God's people as they gather about the Sacrament and receive the body and blood of the Lord, brings God's condemnation upon himself and contributes to weakness and sickliness and sleep in the church (1 Corinthians 11:28-30). Hence Christians must maintain their unity (Ephesians 4:1 ff.), do all things without dissension (Philippians 2:14-16), and maintain their first love for one another no matter how

44

adept they become at rejecting error (Revelation 2:1 ff.); in all these critical situations the pastor is essential for keeping the saving Gospel and the Word of forgiveness at its work (cf. Matthew 18:15-35 and the three previous passages). This fact makes parish preaching and the administration of the Sacrament with the attendant practices for safeguarding thoughtful Communion an intrinsic part of parish administration.

But many other activities of the pastor, obviously, contribute to the functioning of the members of the parish in the spiritual nurture of all. The family stands out as a primary unit (cf. Ephesians 5:22 ff.). Hence every investment of energy in the spiritual nurture of parents, before marriage and child rearing and during it, is essential. Americans like to hire caretakers to take over their responsibilities, and so pastors and teachers easily replace parents in the estimation of the latter. But it is spiritual nurture to get parents to undertake their tasks, to habilitate the family as an organ of spiritual growth, and to help parents counsel together in special training groups and agencies for the purpose. This is much more than marital counseling or family service, for it implies all of the resources of such agencies plus the developing of the skill in using the redeeming work of Christ as promotion of the life in God.

The churches have had much experience in gathering their people according to sex or age levels for special interest groups. These groupings are all to the good, for they set up a matrix for mutual conversation concerning the common problems of the Christian calling. Nor need the pastor hesitate because he thinks that the activity is getting out of hand when it is strongly social and recreational in character; the family is social and recreational too, when it functions properly. But the pastor truly administrates such agencies when he is everlastingly at it to keep Christians at their calling; when he contrives ways by which they stimulate one another to common worship; when he gets them to set aside at least some time for exploring the Bible and what it has to say to their specific concerns; when he leads them to view their common enjoyment and fellowship as a gift of God to be used for God's purposes; and when he utilizes their activities to uncover new gifts of the Spirit in "helps and governments," abilities for serving and leading Godward.

III. Specialized Tasks in Administrating Nurture

Administration does a specialized job when the pastor supervises the activities not just of the congregation in general but of staff personnel in particular. In actual practice such personnel is to a small degree (if at all) salaried, and it is to a great extent volunteer. We are concerned not just with the theory of administrating staff personnel, but with the structure of parish nurture involved in this administration.

Even where the salaried personnel is few or part time, it should become self-evident that the pastor is concerned for the spiritual nurture not merely by this staff, but of it. Daily devotionals and staff meetings to allot tasks and clarify duties and distribute assignments will have their inner core of common worship and feeding on the Word of life. The pastor will, in

46

the nature of his training and office, be concerned for the program of worship, study, and professional growth that leads back into the one thing needful so that it can be properly distributed to others. Much of the rivalry or at least aloofness between pastors and teachers has given way during these years in which the practices of common worship and study have become more general. If the authorities concerned with certificating teachers have brought about a trek of parish school teachers to summer school for continued training, how much busier ought the church's workers, pastors and teachers alike, be in refreshing their own techniques and above all their heart through the Bible and the Word of life. Summer schools, conferences and workshops and institutes, study conferences and correspondence courses, should become rich resources for this spiritual growth of the church's nurturers.

This concern for continued growth and personal nurture applies also to the volunteer and nonprofessional staff of a congregation. The teachers in Sunday and vacation Bible schools get careful briefing in how to give the lesson to their pupils. Often after they have been over the same ground a number of times this instruction becomes boring. But teaching staffs should receive help for their spiritual nurture, which means more than getting hints for teaching lessons or maintaining discipline or visiting delinquent pupils. This help involves common worship and provision of the Word of God applied to personal spiritual growth. A teachers' meeting should be as consciously a device for strengthening the teacher's grasp on God as the Sunday school period should be for the pupil.

The pastor's administration of the teaching staff, professional or volunteer, will be concerned with nurturing their spiritual life. Again it is important that the pastor remember what administration means. He may know a great deal less about classroom teaching than some of the teachers who are in his care. Most pastors continue to learn a great deal about teaching from their veteran lay or professional teachers. But the pastor is through his very call and calling responsible for keeping the helpers of the congregation at their task of nurturing spiritual life. The Sunday school is not operating a mere statistical or token organization; its teachers have to magnify Christ before their pupils. The parish school is not merely holding its own with the public school system, and its plus over the others is not just the better character of its products or the fact that some of them sing in the choir on Sundays; it is an agency for spiritual nurture. This means that its pupils are close to Christ and Him crucified, day by day; that their fellowship in classroom and lunchroom and playground is that of Christians ultimately edifying one another; and that they go back into Christian families in which they make a palpable contribution not just of obedience, but of the Spirit of God through their speech and song about Jesus.

In all of the activities of teachers and the pastor, it is important once more to underscore that the process doesn't end there, but begins a chain reaction. The teacher teaches Christian children so that the children edify, witness, and teach others. The pastor preaches to his congregation so that the members, right in that service and in their homes and callings, speak the call of God to others whether they be Christian or non-Christian. The pastor trains his catechumens, not simply to give the right answers when questioned, or ultimately to be admitted to Holy Communion, but to join the ranks of those who profess their faith and thus move others to love and to good works.

Thus we are prepared to affirm again that the parish nurture which the pastor administrates is never the pouring into a mold, the lining up of people in ranks, or merely the protection from false teaching. But it is the provision for growth. It is more like raising a family or operating a restaurant than it is like manipulating a bulldozer. The pastor leads as he feeds. He leads so that the feeding is more efficient; he leads to where the feeding is going on; he leads so that others feed. The test of his work is not just how many come to listen to him, but what they do when they go into their own callings of life again. Hence the accent of his relation to his people is not simply to get them to listen, even as the Lord Jesus was not satisfied merely with the fact that people heard Him; He had to remind them that the shrewd listeners were those who acted as well as heard. The accent in the pastor's work toward the body of Christ is that the body be sound and that it grow; and the body is individual members working together toward one another and toward their world.

Basically the parish ministry has little time for anything that is not directly applicable to parish nurture. But if the pastor is going to play that role, he himself has to be helped to grow up into Christ; he himself is to labor as servant and shepherd under the Chief Shepherd and the Suffering Servant. Hence the first step in the pastor's administration of parish nurture is that he himself is nurtured daily by the Bread of life, by Gospel and Sacrament, with his people and his family. If, in making this possible, staff and parish elders and wife and children and a father confessor function also toward the pastor, that is the administration of parish nurture in full cycle.

In Christian Giving

As we discussed the pastor at work in guiding his people in worship and through the many structures of Christian nurture, we illustrated the general principles of his feeding and leading by numerous instances of practical effort. We said that the pastor and his co-workers have to be resourceful in devising the individual operations of input of the nurturing word and response of worship, and of output of mutually nurturing action. We now shall single out one of the areas of practical activity in which these operations of nurture and labor go on: Christian giving. In one sense all of the output of Christians is giving; they are giving themselves to God in worship; they are giving themselves to one another in love and cooperation. We shall try to use the term both in that general sense and in the particular one which the average Christian recognizes as right under the surface if not explicit, and that is the giving of money. In the American economy and in the program of the church which

51

has become accepted among us, the normal ingredients
are a full-time salaried pastor, a salaried staff (as soon
as possible), a building to house activities of worship
and Christian education and fellowship, and cooperation with a denomination that shares in a worldwide
program of education and missions; and all of these
take money. Hence the raising of this money is a constant accent in the administration of the standard
parish.

I. Giving Is the Christian's Business

Giving is the Christian's business. Hence it becomes an immediate part of the pastor's work to train
Christians for giving and to guide them in it. Giving
is not simply the churchly counterpart of raising funds
for the work of a secular club or business. But giving
is a gift from God by which God puts His people to
work for Him and for which He empowers them with
His Holy Spirit. Hence the pastor feeds his people
and leads them into this work.

We are fortunate in having a full-dress study of
the administration of Christian giving spread out on
the pages of the New Testament. The church employs
it frequently as it seeks to stimulate its people to the
modern version of liberality for church purposes. It
is important to recognize again and again what the
premises of this giving are; what it is for, and therefore what the parallel purposes in contemporary giving are; and, for our special purpose, what the pastoral
administrator does as he plays his role as feeder and
leader in guiding Christians to give money. The case
study to which we refer is, of course, St. Paul's gather-

ing of a contribution from the churches of Greece and perhaps Asia Minor for the relief of famine in the mother church in Jerusalem. This we view in the two letters to the Corinthians. The principles to be applied to the subject are set out also in the sayings of Jesus and in several epistles of St. Paul not dealing directly with the collection of money for relief.

We can most quickly relate this subject to our preceding discussions when we begin with St. Paul's classifying of the will to give and the capacity for Christian giving as a grace, that is a gift of God to the person who is going to do the giving. We are reminded of 1 Corinthians 12 and its list of powers and activities energized by the Spirit when we read in 2 Corinthians 8:

> We desired Titus that as he had begun, so he would also finish in you the same grace also. Therefore, as ye abound in everything, in faith and utterance and knowledge and in all diligence and in your love to us, see that ye abound in this grace also. (Vv. 6, 7)

That a person gives money to a Christian cause, in this instance for the care of other Christians, is the result of the Holy Spirit at work in him. This at once makes this gift at work in the giver an objective of the church's pastor and feeder. For the gift of the Spirit is, on the one hand, subject to erosion and self-delusion. Then it becomes a danger for the church, and administration becomes the task of unmasking and changing or rejecting it. The story of Ananias and Sapphira is illustrative (Acts 5:1-11). The early Christians in Jerusalem had carried the business of giving

53

for the care of each other into a magnificent over-simplification: they had all things in common (4:32). This was to be the mark of "them that believed." But Ananias and Sapphira tried to be counted in that number, while retaining a part of their property. St. Peter analyzed this in its simplest terms: They lied to the Holy Ghost; they tempted the Spirit of the Lord. Their deficiency was not simply one of love for the needy of the church, or of faith in God; but it was their inner claim that they belonged to God's people when they did not; it was the endeavor to make capital for self-satisfaction in fellowship in the faith out of outward actions which did not accord with the inside intention. They died: thus the church in Jerusalem was protected.

Conversely, it was the nature of the Macedonians who were doing such a good job of Christian giving, prompted by the Spirit, that they "gave their own selves to the Lord, and unto us by the will of God" (2 Corinthians 8:5). They were poor people, but rich in the grace of giving (v. 2). Hence it became the business of administration in the early church to convey their gift to the needy, to build up and make use of that gift also in other Christians, and to use the illustration of the Macedonians as a stimulus for the giving of others. This takes closer examination.

The church quickly builds up administrative machinery for the first of these stages: to convey the gifts of Christians to their destination. Part of this process is to alert the givers concerning the needs for their gifts. 1 Corinthians 16 is often quoted in this process — the suggestions for gathering the money weekly so that it is there to be remitted when the time comes.

The administrative detail for producing the willingness to give the gift, however, is even more interesting and not so frequently discerned. Basic to this phase of giving, in the record of 2 Corinthians, is cultivation of giving as a grace, that is, as a gift of God to the heart of the giver. This process was already at work in Corinth because of the Gospel which St. Paul and Titus had been preaching (8:6), and their objective was to keep bringing this gift in them toward perfection. This is simply the process of Christian nurture which we have previously discussed, and for which the reiteration of the redeeming work of Jesus Christ is of primary importance. 2 Corinthians 8 itself employs this process. St. Paul affirms that he is not operating with the method of command (v. 8). For he is aiming at a sincere love, one that is attached to the work and gift of God, he says; and commandment would cut through and sever this power line. That power line he immediately stressed:

For ye know the grace of our Lord Jesus Christ, that, though He was rich, yet for your sakes He became poor, that ye through His poverty might be rich. (V. 9)

This is a very concise statement; it carries its load in 2 Corinthians because through the whole letter Saint Paul had been restating the redemptive work of Jesus as the heart of his message and the one power which he had to produce effects among them. (Cf. 1:3-5, 18-22; 2:14-17; 3:3-11; 4:4-6, 14-18; 5:10-21; 6:16-18)

At the same time St. Paul enters upon a process which is in the exact sense administration, "oversight." It is here that we gather a most fruitful observation for our present purpose. This is that the example of one group of Christians can stimulate another. Saint Paul holds before the Corinthians the illustration of the Macedonians (2 Corinthians 8:2-5). He points up how remarkable their giving was in that it went beyond what could be rightfully expected. He says that his plea to the Corinthians is linked with the zeal of the Macedonians; their energy and consecration is to play a part in giving which commandment, personal authority and plea, cannot and should not achieve. (V. 8)

St. Paul at once aligns with the pressure of this example the character of two other men, administrators in our language: Titus and possibly Luke. He says that the manner of Titus' work toward and for them is not a display of exerting himself by commandment; it is rather a display of his love for people and his zeal for their Christian progress. These men had a reputation for zealous preaching of the Gospel and for scrupulous dealing with other people's money. These men were not merely good handlers of money; they were a stimulus to giving.

Furthermore, the grace of giving at work in the Corinthians themselves was to become a stimulus to the giving of others; in fact, it had already become so; "your zeal hath provoked very many" (2 Corinthians 9:2). Their own past record is one which had made other Christians zealous, and it was important that they should not flag and thus fail to give this potent stimulus in the future. The Phillips paraphrase points up some of the very unabashed encouragement — fund raisers call it needling — which St. Paul employs:

. . . I know it is really quite superfluous for me to be writing to you about this matter of giving to fellow Christians, for I know how willing you are. Indeed I have told the Macedonians with some pride that "Achaia was ready to undertake this service a twelvemonth ago." Your enthusiasm has consequently been a stimulus to many of them. I am, however, sending the brothers just to make sure that our pride in you is not unjustified. For, between ourselves, it would never do if some of the Macedonians were to accompany me on my visit to you and find you unprepared for this act of generosity! We (not to speak of you) should be horribly ashamed, just because we had been so proud and confident of you. This is my reason, then, for urging the brothers to visit you before I come myself, so that they can get your promised gift ready in good time. But, having let you into my confidence, I should like it to be a spontaneous gift, and not money squeezed out of you by what I have said. All I will say is that poor sowing means a poor harvest, and generous sowing means a generous harvest. Let everyone give as his heart tells him, neither grudgingly nor under compulsion, for God loves the man whose heart is in his gift. (2 Corinthians 9:1-7)

This impulse toward prompt and continued giving could certainly degenerate into simple personal pressure. Hence St. Paul promptly returns to the reinforcement of the spiritual source:

God is able to make all grace abound toward you; that ye, always having all sufficiency in all things, may abound to every good work (as it is written: He hath dispersed abroad; he hath given to the poor; his righteousness remaineth forever. Now He that ministereth seed to the sower both minister bread for your food and multiply your seed sown and increase the fruits of your righteousness), being enriched in everything to all bountifulness, which causeth through us thanksgiving to God. (2 Corinthians 9: 8-11 AV)

The point important for our concern is that giving is brought into the orbit of a mutual activity, and the apostle-pastor is a promoter not just of the giving, but of the mutual encouragement to giving and display of what true giving is, the "fellowship of the ministering to the saints." (2 Corinthians 8:4)

As we survey this New Testament study of giving, we are led to one important question: Is the grace of giving one in which the Christian basically proves his love to God, or his love to people, or both? Are we concerned here with a gift that is basically worship, and does the administration of it prompt to that universal consecration and service to God which is the Christian's true life, or are we concerned with evoking acts of love to people? The account in 2 Corinthians concerns the gathering of money for a project of charity and welfare to needy people; but is that just an exception to a more general rule? As the pastor administrates the parish, does he prime his people to give because they love one another and other people, or does he prime them to give because they love and worship God? If we now consider the ancient offer-

58

tory, with its bringing to the altar of the bread and wine for the sacrament, to be the bringing of the congregation's gifts, and if we thus relate giving to an act of worship, how can we speak of the giving of our members as being a motivation for others? Isn't the faith which is our offering in worship invisible?

These questions are due to oversimplifications which tend to creep into popular theology; they come in part through the zeal of those who are trying to stimulate their members to giving, in part through the fleshly defenses against such stimulation which are set up by the people who are the targets of it. Actually worship and love for people are not alternative motives to giving. Certainly all of our labors with which we take care of people, even with our taxes, all of them (whether carried out with benefit of ceremonies in church services or not) are our reasonable service to God. We do well to distinguish in our minds between life as worship and church services as worship; the latter are hours set aside from the rest of life in which we adore God together with His people and find the power to dedicate our entire lives to God in a reasonable service.

Let us remember that in the scheme of the Christian religion love, whether love to God or love to people, isn't a motive at all. Love is action, it is already that to which men are motivated. We would be helpless people indeed if the motive power for our actions had to be simply power derived from our own selves. "Herein is love," says St. John, and he is talking about our love for people, "not that we loved God, but that He loved us" (1 John 4:10). When we give

59

money as an act of worship, the power for this does not come from our love to God, but it comes from God capturing us and making us His own through Jesus Christ; our gifts are simply a token of the fact that we belong to Him and are our way of telling one another that we do. When we give money for people, our love for the people whom we are helping is God's own gift into the heart through Jesus Christ the Savior.

For love to God and love to people are both the work of God in our hearts. Nor will you find one there and the other missing; the person who claims to love God and forgets to love people probably doesn't love God at all. (1 John 3:11-18)

But this means that we shall not be anxious to discover a kind of giving of money which is an act of love to God and *not* an act of love to people. Basically God can't be loved by giving Him money anyway, or by building buildings to Him; "the Lord is not worshiped in temples built with hands" (Acts 17:24b-25, altered; cf. also 2 Chronicles 6:18ff.; John 4:23, 24). Our Lord was much concerned over the invasion of the life of God in the heart of man by the processes of physical living; and so He was concerned about the right use of money, "the mammon of unrighteousness" and legal tender for the life divorced from the Spirit of God. In His great parable on the subject, the unjust steward (Luke 16:1-13), He describes the wisdom about money that God's man must have to be as smart and shrewd in its use as the man without God. The man without God will use money, if he is smart, to produce human relations that last beyond the present moment. Even in terms of unsanctified common sense the man without that kind of shrewdness is really a fool. But the man shrewd in the way that God would have him to be does something with his money also for the life of the Spirit of God. He recognizes that sooner or later he comes into judgment for the use of his money, and life must therefore be more than mere amassing of wealth and enjoyment of it (Luke 16:19-31, Rich Man and Lazarus, against the avarice of the Pharisees; or the Rich Fool, Luke 12:16-21). But more than that: the wise use of money this side of the grave is that with it and by means of it you "make friends" who will "receive you into everlasting habitations" (Luke 16:9). Jesus herewith focuses on the human beings with whom we are related in a life that transcends that of physical existence. They are to be our friends — in His definition that is people who give up their lives for us and for whom we give up our lives. That is His picture for the body of Christ, the aggregate of Christians in a given place who are responsible for one another. That is the function of money, the one thing that money, legal tender for physical life, can do for the life that is of the eternal variety: it can contribute toward people's being members of the body of Christ.

Our first reaction to Jesus' parable about the mammon of unrighteousness is that we can spend our money on people in such a way that we meet them in the world beyond the grave, "when we fail" (Luke 16:9). Yet our Lord never drew too sharp a distinction between God's kind of life this side of the grave and the other side; it exists on both sides. Hence, to lay up treasure for ourselves where moth and rust do not corrupt can mean as much the care for the spiritual life of people before death as after. (Matthew 6:19ff.)

Therefore the great objective of money, in Jesus' thinking, is the spiritual life of people. Our question about 2 Corinthians 8 and St. Paul's counsel on giving, therefore, is not: Is giving for welfare the only kind of giving or can there be giving also for God? But the question should be: What giving is simultaneously helping people and serving the purposes of God? When we have the answer to that question we know what the objective of the administration of Christian giving should be. And the answer is: giving by which people are placed and kept in the realm of God, Christian care climaxing in the sharing of the Gospel. Thus our Lord describes the career of the people who, at judgment day, will be adjudged as having lived the life that enters upon eternal life in heaven: they will have been people who fed and clothed, visited and comforted God's people (Matt. 25:34-40). This does not mean that they were deliberately hardhearted to other people; Christians are those who, while there is opportunity, do good to all men — but especially to them who are of the household of faith (Gal. 6:10). This is the ultimate faithfulness which Jesus wants to have His disciples practice already in this present world, that they might be given charge over the greater tasks of the world to come (Luke 12). And this is what makes the pastoral care for people with reference to money a compound of administration: The pastor leads people to invest in each other's spiritual welfare; and he supervises the activity by which they lead one another to make that investment.

II. The Pastor Equips People for Christian Giving

We are now ready to describe pastoral labors by which people are led and fed to give as Christians. All of these operations involve: training people to *give* as an act of the heart, out of the Christian will of love and toward people in their need; training people to give as an act of faith, out of consecration to God and for the carrying out of God's purposes; training people *to help one another to these goals.*

The pastor has to help his people respect money and the earning of it. It does not make for Christian giving to cheapen money; it does not make for Christian faithfulness to belittle the earning of money or the giving of it. True, it is an objective of Christian nurture, we said, to enhance the callings, also those in which Christians earn money, and therefore any dishonesty in acquiring it is bad and all prizing of honest earning good.

> Let him that stole steal no more; but rather let him labor, working with his hands the thing which is good, that he may have to give to him that needeth. (Ephesians 4:28)

But some of this respect has to be ingrained by helping to recognize the obstacles to the proper attitude toward money. The human heart becomes impressed by the standards which life without the Spirit of God sets; these standards are enforced by ordinary living, getting ahead in the world, and having fun and recreation. Everything that the parish can do for its families and family nurture is essential for the proper standards of the growing generation. The children

63

of the family have to be helped to learn the importance of the mutual concern of the members of the family: when they do things to help, when they do things for money, what they do with allowances, and how the Christian family has to differ from the non-Christian family in money matters. The family is the great training ground for discerning the maladies of worry, of self-indulgence, of status-seeking, and for learning first-hand the importance of contentment, of family-feeling and sharing, of satisfaction with less expensive but more substantial values in the home and occupation.

This functioning of parents and the Christian home is an objective of pastoral concerning and training. It is fundamental for any further training in Christian giving. Only as children see the basis for mutual care in the family, the parental handling of such money problems as household expenses, financing the home, paying the taxes, supplying cash for school and education, will the next stage of Christian giving become clearer, namely, contributing money to the church. For the first investment of Christians in making friends with the mammon of unrighteousness goes on within the family. How money can be given to the church for the spiritual care of people has to be learned first of all in the family. How the church interprets giving to the parish budget or to Synod will make sense only as Christians have learned, in also the secular walks of life, what it means to give money so that people are nurtured for God and kept with Him.

Good administration of parish giving and fund raising implies the most careful interpretation to every giver of what the money is for: that it is actually to be devoted to the task of making friends in heavenly habitations. True, the giving is going to be an act of consecration to God; but consecration is not a motive for giving, it is the giving itself. Christians have to be helped to understand that the money which is gathered in regular contributions provides for the pastoral and teaching ministry to the members of the congregation and community. They have to see why it is important to share with the teacher in all good things, namely, as part of the program of restoring hampered people to spiritual life, and as direct help to the teaching member of the church (Gal. 6:1-10). They are to understand why the congregation equips and maintains buildings, namely, that people, young and old, may be helped to focus their minds on God in worship and be nurtured in the Word of Christ. They have to be given insight into the many treasuries which draw on the contributions of the average parish, insight in terms of human beings who are reached: the needy through the charities of the community, weaker congregations of the area who are being helped to become independent, non-Christians who are being evangelized in American communities or reached with the Gospel in areas overseas, and the many fellow Christians throughout the world who are going to be benefited by the church's workers who are being trained in the educational system of the church.

As the members of the congregation are led to this insight, the ground is prepared for actually implementing the motive power necessary for the actual giving. Again this power is "not by commandment"; it cannot be by prescription. But it must be as response of love for men which comes from the love of God to us. St. Paul points out that where Christians deliberately withhold their support from the care of those of their own household, they "have denied the faith and are worse than infidels" (1 Timothy 5:8). Conversely, people who are going to give to the church's work must understand that their own hearts have been released from the selfishness of fleshly indulgence and irresponsibility toward others by the redeeming work of Jesus Christ, that they have been implanted in the company of God's people, who live with God's own kind of life in a world that transcends present time, and that therefore their investment in the life of the Spirit of God is all-important.

In all of this the amount of giving receives attention, not in terms of prescriptions and quotas, but in terms of the will to give to the needs of human beings.

Now therefore perform the doing of it, that as
there was a readiness to will, so there may be
a performance also out of that which ye have.
For if there be first a willing mind, it is accepted
according to that a man hath and not according
to that he hath not. (2 Corinthians 8:11, 12)

The power for that giving is the grace of God, the very grace with which Jesus Christ gave Himself. (2 Corinthians 8:9)

This axiom is basic for operating one of the outstanding devices of parish administration of Christian giving: the sharing of information about performances. Parishes quite generally tried this in the report of annual contributions and many have given it up either because some deemed it an invasion of their privacy or others felt that it put a secular or fleshly leverage into the compulsion for giving. Recently much has been made of the sharing of performance in the actual promotion of giving at the level of initial subscriptions. The Kurth-Zehnder variation of the plan enlists workers on a comparable income level actually to assert to one another what their own level of giving is going to be, as part of the program of suggesting the size of the gift. This plan has come under much adverse criticism, and it can probably be administered in a way that stresses shame for poor performance as the motivation for giving. Properly handled, it should work well within the Christian framework, but this implies these essentials: that the workers, beginning with the pastor and chairman down through the individual solicitors, are utterly committed and sincere about their own giving and to that end draw amply on the message of Christ's redeeming work for their own motivation; that as many workers as possible are mobilized and evangelized in the solicitation program; that the solicitation of the prospect by the worker never degenerate to the simple request for a subscription or handing on of the parish plea for funds, but that there be always the exchange of the Word of the redeeming work of Christ. Only so will the sample of the worker's effort be interpreted, not as a gouge for giving, but as the example, itself empowered by the grace of Christ, which sets a pattern for the grace of the person solicited.

In Christian giving one of the greatest obstacles to any program of administration is the hidden factor in the life of every Christian concerning his capacity for giving. Income is obviously not a sufficient criterion, for persons differ widely in the responsibilities for people which they share. But the really hidden factor is the status of a given Christian's spiritual life and his readiness for giving. The battle of flesh with the Spirit in the heart of every Christian makes it unlikely that any gift will ever be given wholly from motives of the Spirit, and some flesh will influence, either for the larger or smaller, the size of the contribution. In the practical working of a given parish the assumption is usually made that those who are giving very little or nothing are at the bottom of the heap, spiritually. What shall be done? The pastor or finance committee is not endowed with the prescience of St. Peter to tell the small giver that he is lying to the Holy Ghost; maybe he isn't lying, or he may actually be one whose spiritual development has been terribly hampered. Nor can these administrators speak up to a larger giver that the gift is insufficient and the very munificence of it is a sham. What is good administration in these cases?

The answer is that the program of spiritual nurture, discussed previously, remains basic. A parishwide program of Christian giving can be a great spiritual stimulus to a congregation, not because giving makes stronger, but because that which properly makes for giving, namely, the mutual discussing of the redeeming work of Jesus Christ and common worship, makes for spiritual life and because the more active people are in promoting spiritual life, the more substantial the congregation is going to be. The rule of thumb set up in many a parish is: there should be more campaigns for Bible study, or family worship, or mutual Christian fellowship, operating in a parish than campaigns for the raising of funds. By campaigns we mean not simply letters, for that is hardly administration, but programs in which as many different members of the church as possible speak to the rest of them. To this end the entire congregation has to become an agency for summoning one another to prayer and to the use of Gospel and Sacrament.

Where the parish is busy in recruiting new members, the special problem enters of how to break the news to newcomers that the church asks for a great deal of money. This problem can be solved only on the level of the training classes and initial discussions of the Christian religion. There it is that newcomers to the church have to be helped to understand why the church asks for money, where the will is to come from to give it, what the purposes of it are, and what the size of the contribution is to be. Actually the new members of the church are often not as much a problem as the veterans who have learned to steel their hearts against the pleas for cash and whose hearts need a reopening to the love of God to them. A greater difficulty is the program of admitting child confirmees to membership and to a share in the regular giving of the congregation. Often they are below the age of making money of their own; if their parents are unchurched, their allowances, if any, seem unsuitable for Christian giving. Here the projects of youth groups and the impressing of the meaning and purpose of giving become of special importance.

To mobilize a congregation so that most of its work, corporately and in its societies, revolves around gathering money for various debts is a possible arrangement, but it does not seem to us to be the pastoral task. For the pastor leads and feeds. The old gag of the fund raiser that the sheep are pastured in order to be shorn several times a year squeezes the parable beyond its point. The pastor is in the business of giving men eternal life through Jesus Christ, and of guiding people so that they share that ministry. Christian giving should leave the giver stronger in grace than he had been. To that end he must consume the grace of Christ.

In Community Witness

The Christian lives in the world for a purpose. That he is saved for everlasting life is not this purpose, but rather a step in the direction of this purpose. The purpose is that he bear witness of God, display Him to others, confess Him before men, make His name and praise glorious, be His image, and love others as God first loved him. The very profusion of these terms in Holy Writ indicates how pervasive and comprehensive this purpose of God's man in the world is. But if this is true, then the pastor is in a crucial position to be the trainer of witnesses, an overseer and administrator of witnesses at work. We have surveyed the administration of what might be called the internal witness, the oversight of Christians functioning to build up one another within the congregation. In this chapter we are concerned with the witness of Christians toward the community.

I. The Church and Witness

From the beginning it is important to keep from oversimplifying our subject. Frequently the process of the Gospel is thought of as drawing an individual in the world into communion with the heavenly Father and the Lord Jesus through the work of the Holy Spirit. That this individual is related to a church is thought of only in institutional or statistical terms. Likewise the process of witness is thought of as an individual playing his role in bringing the saving Gospel to the needy individual, and when the Gospel has taken root the task is done; again the church is incidental to the picture. The New Testament, in contrast, relates the coming of the Gospel to the work of the church; it puts the new convert into the context of the church, and it makes witnessing an act of people who are related to the church as members and bearers of the church's faith and Word to their world. This is important for our subject, for the pastor is God's gift to the church, given so that he might train the entire church which is under his care to witness to its surrounding community.

Let us review what we mean by the Christian's witness. The basic Scripture is Jesus' word to His disciples on the evening of the first Easter (Luke 24: 44-48):

Then He said to them, "This is what I told you when I was still with you — that everything that is written about Me in the Law of Moses and the Prophets and the Psalms must come true." Then He opened their minds to the understanding of the Scriptures and said to them, "The

Scriptures said that Christ should suffer as He has done and rise from the dead on the third day and that repentance leading to the forgiveness of sins should be preached to all the heathen in His name. You are to be witnesses to all this [Acts 1:8: My witnesses], beginning at Jerusalem. And I will send down upon you what My Father has promised. Wait here in the city until you are clothed with power from on high." (Goodspeed)

Here the followers of Jesus Christ are portrayed as people who are observing a certain process by themselves playing a part in it, a process set forth in the Scriptures of the Old Testament as one by which God Himself turned men to Himself and His forgiveness of their sins. The process revolves about God's sending of His Son the Messiah, who would suffer and die and rise again to work out this forgiveness of man's sin. The process reaches its targets: the people right there where the first disciples heard this word; and by the message and proclamation of this Christ and His work first carried on by these first followers and transplanted to all who hear it reaches out from there to men throughout the world regardless of birth. Thus the first disciples were witnesses not only in having been physically able to see Jesus Christ in the flesh or to observe the details of the crucifixion and resurrection but especially in proclaiming God's plan in Christ so that men would turn from sin to forgiveness. Their competence for witness depended not merely on the chance that they were in the locality of these great

73

events and had their eyes open but on the gift of God from on high, the endowment with God's own Spirit.

From this we see that a witness in any age is one who himself has been turned to the forgiveness of sins by the great fact of Christ's death and resurrection, and who now speaks the message of that work of Christ on to his world. The church has often stressed that the behavior of the witness must be a potent element in this process, and that is true. St. Paul affirmed that he behaved himself in keeping with the Gospel which he preached (2 Corinthians 4:2) and urged that the people to whom he wrote might likewise walk in keeping with their call and the Gospel (Ephesians 4:1; 5:2; Colossians 1:10; 2:6; 1 Thessalonians 2:12); especially toward those who did not yet accept the Gospel (Colossians 4:5; 1 Thessalonians 4:12). This counterpart of the Gospel in behavior is always an accompaniment of the Gospel, a Gospel which is actually being spoken.

> . . . The word is nigh thee, even in thy mouth, and in thy heart: that is, the word of faith which we preach: that if thou shalt confess with thy mouth the Lord Jesus and shalt believe in thine heart that God hath raised Him from the dead thou shalt be saved. (Romans 10:8, 9)

The outspeech of Jesus' redeeming work is an essential correlate of the Christian's faith and life. The highest act to which the term "witness" can be applied is the demonstration of faith which speaks the Gospel also when in danger of death or at the expense of life — just as Jesus witnessed before Pontius Pilate. (1 Timothy 6:13; Revelation 17:6)

74

This is the witness to which the Christian devotes himself when he becomes a member of the Christian church. In fact, the situation that he is a witness at all is due to this membership. For the message that moved him to repentance came to him from members in the holy Christian church who had in turn received that message and had been led to repentance through others. Our Lord links the unity of His disciples and witnesses together with their invasion of the world with His Word:

Consecrate them by truth. Your message is truth. Just as You sent Me to the world, I have sent them to the world. And it is for their sake that I consecrate Myself, that they also may be consecrated by truth. It is not for them only that I make this request. It is also for those who through their message come to believe in Me. Let them all be one. Just as You, Father, are in union with Me and I am with You, let them be in union with Us, so that the world may believe that You sent Me. I have given them the glory that You gave Me so that they may be one just as We are, I in union with them and You with Me, so that they may be perfectly unified and the world may recognize that You sent Me and that You love them just as You loved Me. (John 17:17-24 Goodspeed)

St. Paul makes the same connection between the unity of the witnessing group and their witness to one another and their world:

I, the prisoner for the Lord's sake, appeal to you to live lives worthy of the summons you have received; with perfect humility and gentleness, with patience, bearing with one another lovingly. Make every effort to maintain the unity of the Spirit through the tie of peace. (Ephesians 4:1, 2)

Do everything without any grumbling or disputing so that you will be blameless and honest, faultless children of God in the midst of a crooked and perverted age, in which you appear like stars in a dark world offering men the message of life. Then I will have reason to boast of you on the Day of Christ, because my exertion and labor have not been wasted. (Philippians 2:14-16 Goodspeed)

"Unity," with reference to the Christian church, always implies the picture of the body of Christ, the interrelation and fellowship of its members by which they intercommunicate the life and Spirit of God toward one another. Hence the Christian witness speaks as he is empowered by his fellow Christians. Their word to him becomes his work to them and to others.

Now I beseech you brethren, by the name of our Lord Jesus Christ, that ye all speak the same thing and that there be no divisions among you, but that ye be perfectly joined together in the same mind and in the same judgment. (1 Corinthians 1:10 AV)

Only let your conversation be as it becometh the Gospel of Christ, that whether I come and see you or else be absent, I may hear of your affairs, that ye stand fast in one spirit, with one mind striving together for the faith of the Gospel. (Philippians 1:27 AV)

This unity is never mere accord, absence of bickering, but always common affirmation and telling of the Gospel. St. Paul frequently speaks of the "fellowship of the Gospel," e. g., Philippians 1:3-7:

> I thank my God upon every remembrance of you . . . for your fellowship in the Gospel from the first day unto now . . . inasmuch as both in my bonds and in the defence and confirmation of the Gospel ye are all partakers of my grace.

As the Christian church faces the surrounding community, it needs to present a united front. All Christians have to set forth their faith in Jesus Christ in the same way; there can be no spectacle of division makers or confusion of the essence of that Gospel: that Jesus Christ is Savior and Lord (cf. Galatians 1:8; 1 John 4:1-3). But there must also be a united front of good will to the world round about. Christians are fishers of men, and the powerful witness which they throw out over the world is precisely the same which our Lord made available to human hearts: the witness to God's faithful redemption by the suffering and death and rising of Jesus (John 18:36, 37). Where one falters, the unbelief of the world and the conspiracy of the devil have a chance to break through and make inroads. Christians in a community are like a lifesaving operation in which a band of searchers try to find a lost child in the forest. They have to march through the woods hand in hand; and where somebody breaks the chain, the entire operation comes short of its purpose.

Here then is the pastor's task. The quotations from the epistles of St. Paul which have illustrated the church's fellowship of speaking the Gospel to its world are all a part of the apostle's pastoral enterprise, an effort to stimulate and strengthen his readers to their share in the program. We saw how he was concerned with every detail of the process, beginning with the unity and accord of their own members in their own communion; he was concerned with the kindness and helpfulness of their speech to non-Christians, with the sincerity and consistency of their conduct, and with their apparent will to self-sacrifice and helpfulness toward Christian and non-Christian alike. But he was also concerned with providing the means and prescribing the continued use of the means by which this witness could be begun and supported. This was the word of Jesus Christ, the name of Jesus Christ, the Gospel of Jesus Christ, remembered also for themselves and not merely expressed toward others. In other words: the witness of Christians to their communities and their world needed the constant resource of the remembered work of Jesus Christ, His suffering and death and resurrection. The remembrance of this work was to go on in their common worship, in their fellowship in their families and friendships, through their participation in the Lord's Supper, in the recollection of their baptism, in their review of the Gospel which he himself had preached to them and which his associates were now reviewing with them by means of the letters which he was writing.

What is administrative about this picture is that the apostles guide their fellow Christians into operations which they share and which they stimulate one another to perform, "with one mind striving together for the faith of the Gospel." They need to exert this

78

mutual encouragement because there are obstacles. St. Paul himself was mightily cheered by his Christian friends in the midst of his obstacles and so he expected that their striving together with one mind would mean that they were

> in nothing terrified by . . . adversaries: which is to them an evident token of perdition [i. e., the Gospel] but to you of salvation and that of God. For unto you it is given in the behalf of Christ not only to believe on Him but also to suffer for His sake, having the same conflict which ye saw in me, and now hear to be in me. (Philippians 1:27-30)

II. THE COMPONENTS OF TOTAL PARISH ACTION

In administrating the church's program of witness, the pastor and the leaders of the church need to set up a front which includes all members of the church and all activities of the church. For the strategy toward the outside world makes unceasing demands on the consistency and sincerity of the entire band of Christians. This involves a united front with Christians of other congregations and denominations also. Of that we shall say a bit more later; now we need to concentrate on the operation for which the pastor has been made uniquely responsible, the leading and feeding of the specific group of Christians called his congregation.

Again leading and feeding dare not be dissociated. The pastor guides his people into operations whereby they witness to their communities; but he does so only as he brings God's own energy to bear upon their effort and as he helps all to speak the empowering

Word to one another. This means that the congregation cannot afford to think of some of its activities as intramural, for the community has access to almost all of them, directly or indirectly. It cannot afford to regard some of its activities as approaching the secular and therefore more open to the community, for that would be to say that the warmth of its approach to its community is in inverse ratio to how religious it is.

The church puts up buildings which draw the public eye and advertises services and other functions over which it posts the invitation, "All welcome." For many pastors the guest register becomes the list of most promising prospects for evangelism. The Sunday bulletin carries special invitations to the unchurched in the audience. Many parishes broadcast their Sunday morning services over the radio — a few by television. Is there any field for administration in any of this, other than that involved in plant management and the routines of conducting the service?

A great deal. The number of people from the community who respond to these invitations, or even who listen to broadcasts wholly on their own impulse, is very tiny. The great majority are stimulated to interest through some personal reinforcement: the invitation of a friend or relative or the recollection of the good will of a neighbor. Where people come, on the other hand, only out of curiosity or because of the prestige of a speaker or of the musical program of the church, the barriers against an intelligent and searching interest in the Christian Gospel are formidable. Hence the entire congregation has to be recruited to ply the task of witness outside church hours within homes and workshops and neighborhood contacts; and there they are to represent the church service as a notable meeting in which people are led to confront the living God and receive His mercy for their lives now and future. Next, every worshiper has to be recruited to become a person who in the act and hour of worship gives a demonstration of what true Christian worship is — through his own air of adoration, participation, and search for the Word of life; and he becomes one who, finally, shows tactful and spiritual concern for the visitor in the room whom he does not know and whom he wants to make a shareholder in the Word of life. The larger the church, the more specialized these tasks of welcoming become (if they are not to be overlooked); but the earnestness and manifest sincerity of Christian participants in worship has to be uniform and general if the church is to give genuine witness; for this the pastor has to be leader and feeder.

As a footnote we might comment on broadcasts of regular church services. These are obviously of great value to members of the church unable to attend a given service. They have almost no significance as witness to the non-Christian, however, unless the continuity of the broadcast provides for welcome to nonmembers couched and spoken in such a way that it does not sound perfunctory; unless the difficult portions of the church service receive a special commentary that reveals the concern of the members of the church that everything be understood; unless portions of the service that have meaning only to those present in the church building — such as frequent baptisms or long files of communions — are replaced by commentary for the listening audience; and unless the church announces avenues through which the service of its staff and people are made available to listeners by mail and in person. The devising of a program that will follow through on such arrangements is administration of witness.

The educational activities of the church are fruitful areas for witness to the community, provided that the members of the church are recruited to play their role in attendance, intelligent participation, invitation, and conference with non-Christians. The most common agency is the membership forum for adults which is often attended by friends or relatives of candidates for membership. Many a parish has elaborate provision for teams of visitors to enter homes of Sunday school pupils or to follow up notices of new homes purchased in the community or to bring cheer to sick or needy on the periphery of the congregation. These are splendid, but here enters the pastor's responsibility of leading not merely programs of friendly visiting, but operations of witness. The full value and significance of these calls obtains only as the whole word of life in Christ can be transmitted, gently and briefly perhaps, but nevertheless sincerely. Where omitted, the person visited gains the impression that church members are friendly people but basically like the men at the union or the Elks, and curiously shy about what makes them church people.

The number-one operation of witness arises in the Christian callings, and we have already discussed how the pastor is to feed and lead his people so that they stay in their callings and keep the word of life coming to those who are near them. At first sight this seems an impossible assignment; for life is organic and the relation of the church to individual walks of life seems very remote indeed. Yet even in the practice of the average congregation the possibilities of pastoral nurture of individual callings are under way. Again we note the importance of the Christian family. Here is headquarters for outreach to neighbors, participation in the activities of the neighborhood playground and, in some instances, the neighborhood school. The pastor can bring the techniques of Gospel-sharing to the men and women of special and parent groups; he can supervise the program of education by which the church schools stimulate their pupils to speak the word for Christ wherever this is possible and by which their own families, in turn, are activated to do this speaking. The Christian day school becomes a powerhouse — right through entree into its family group — for promoting community witness.

But more, the educational program of the church helps Christians to see what their opportunities are for speaking the Gospel of God to the people of the community. As children are pointed to their parents' breadwinning occupations and made aware of their parents' contacts with people at work, the methods of displaying the repentant heart and speaking the reason of the hope that is within us become a matter of training. This educational program is carried on not only in the church's schools, but also in the special age and interest groups. A simpler, more parochial era was content with a ladies' aid society that quilted and gave a church dinner from time to time. But with the entering of our people into community life, Christian women are interested in the problems of the community and the modes of bringing Christian witness to bear upon these problems. A group of church women thus becomes a potent arena for administrating training to speak the way of life to friends and neighbors and to make the Christian way apparent in the service groups and activities of the community where the church's women serve. Likewise the men's group will find a special interest and a welcome change from dartball to conversation with one another on the opportunities and techniques for the Christian witness via the channels of service of many kinds in which their members function in their area.

Churches sometimes complain that they have so few people active in public life, even in American communities where they have a sizable proportion of the population as members. But the pastor is to be concerned not merely that he have his members in the public eye. He is to be concerned with what the public eye sees in his members. To that end he has to be unremitting in his efforts to shape the character and the speech of his people (beginning in their youth) so that they have the courage and the ability to say the helpful word and show the way of life in Christ whenever the opportunity presents itself. That opportunity is not always there. But the moment questions of right and wrong are involved, the moment difficulties confront the community, the moment calamity and discouragement beset individuals and groups, that moment Christian love rises to the occasion and the

84

reason for Christian love becomes verbal. Or — it should. In order that his people learn to overcome their reticence and awkwardness, the pastor trains his people that through many occasions for discussion among friends and fellow Christians they put the Christian message into words and thus proclaim repentance toward the forgiveness of sins.

III. Special Projects of the Parish

Many churches have an extensive program of community evangelistic outreach. A few details pertaining to the pastoral administration of these programs should be observed. Again the pastor is to be concerned for parishwide activity which continues with sincerity and persistence after the special endeavor is past, activity which not merely has people inviting to services or making surveys, but also trains them during special activities and otherwise to speak the word that genuinely witnesses to Christ.

The details of administrating the PTR (Preaching-Teaching-Reaching) program have been discussed elsewhere. Here let us view involvement of the theology of parish administration. The PTR program is notable in that it provides an opportunity for expressly developing people through training and mutual discussion. Basic to this must be the review of God's plan in Christ as set forth in the Bible. Here is leading that is simultaneously feeding. The Mission to Ministers which has been a helpful unit of all major PTR endeavors has repeatedly been a great source of spiritual revitalization for participating pastors. But identical blessing emerges also for the members of the congregations. It is important that the evangelism committees (or whatever the units are named that continue operating in the parish after the major effort is completed) receive constant supply from the Gospel and engage in the mutual stimulus of talking this supply; this program is for the pastor to administrate.

Another major use to which this training program can be put is the study and analysis of obstacles besetting the witness in his contacts with the community. This means reviewing the standard lists of approaches and methods for circumventing the apathy or antagonism of some individuals. But much more significant is the opportunity to review the sluggishness of the Christian's heart about carrying out his witness to the community. Where a group of Christians can be trained to face their personal lag and overcome it with new intake of the Spirit, the results will be apparent not just in a project of visiting the community or certain prospects, but also in the improved freedom and kindly boldness with which Christians will speak in their regular callings.

The outstanding contribution of parish training programs for evangelism is in helping people to talk about the way of life through Jesus Christ. Here Christians are notoriously tongue-tied, especially in a denomination where the pastor is traditionally sole spokesman. As the pastor administrates this program of training he leads and feeds. For he guides people to speak up, and he has them practice on one another and in their families. Thus he oversees a program of witness that pervades his own Christian group first of all. To that end he has to feed, for people have to discover that talking about Jesus is never merely saying words previously memorized, but it is always finding the words to describe an event that has already been going on inside the witness himself. And where that event has not been going on, it becomes the function of the entire membership in all of the activities of the church to bring the knowledge of God in Christ Jesus up to a palpable and genuinely experienced level.

The training program for an evangelistic effort in the church is one of the most explicit methods for cultivating witness in the family, out in the bread-winning jobs, and in the neighborhood relations which we have already discussed. Every training program for evangelism has to traverse the entire front of the congregation and help the prospective witnesses see how every sector of the church's operation has to be welded into one Operation Gospel, so that any individual invitation becomes the business of every other Christian to reinforce. Thus it was that the first Christians functioned at Jerusalem; their apostles preached in the public rooms of the temple; the hostility of individuals toward the Gospel was broken down as the Christians themselves infiltrating the throng and the community "magnified them; and men and women in increasing numbers believed in the Lord and joined them." (Acts 5:13, 14 AV and Goodspeed)

As an example of publicity endeavor, The Lutheran Church — Missouri Synod is favorably known among other Christian groups in the United States for its use of mass media and public relations. It is important that a Lutheran pastor administrate the individual parish so that these efforts, many of them national in scope, are actually Christian witness and not merely denominational advertising. The Gospel message of The Lutheran Hour or the Gospel statement and invitation on "This Is the Life" or the paid ad in the Saturday morning paper is going to be witness only as readers and viewers are helped to discover that human beings within their own community actually have been moved by this statement already before it was made. Hence the church's telemission program is crucial in that it corroborates the message of the broadcast by the personal concern of at least one other individual.

It is important that every pastor administrate a program by which all of his members can speak the word which the broadcasts speak; that they can articulate the message to which the press notice invites; that they display an urgent and friendly concern for the people who are coming within the orbit of these media. The Gospel does not work ex opere operato: It is not operative merely because it is there, but it has to be confessed and preached, men have to plead it and witness it. The Word of mass media likewise has to be magnified by individual people. The pastor leads and feeds his people to bring that amplification.

With reference to Lutherans, the sign "The Church of the Lutheran Hour" on a front lawn is ludicrous to the non-Christian public if the people who worship in the building behind it spend their week as though The Lutheran Hour did not exist, and as though the God whom it discusses is penned up in the building.

The good will of the community, the commodity which our day makes purchasable through public relations, is ultimately only for people; the community is merely people in interaction. This does not mean that the building should be neglected or the printed matter shabby; building and printed matter have to reflect taste and a concern for God and people which is corroborated by the entire membership. One church member who comes to church only on Easter devaluates a hundred-dollar advertisement inviting the community to an Easter service. And if the chance visitor lured by that advertisement finds the service incomprehensible and the people frozen, the net worth of the ad approaches zero. Hence the pastor has to train his people (through the Gospel applied to themselves) to support the Gospel of their church.

What of the witness of the Christians of a congregation toward Christians who are not members of their congregation? Where there are a number of congregations of a synod in a community, there should be a great deal of pastoral activity going on by which all the members of all the parishes accept a common responsibility to their community and are fed with the Gospel to the end that they present as united a front across the whole group as each parish must present for itself. This probably goes without saying; it is good to see rivalries and competition between parishes of one communion give way to the inspiration and labor of a combined school program or PTR, or to see a council that puts its members to work in genuine witness. (Incidentally, making a lot of noise in a neighborhood about pornographic literature may be important and necessary, but it is not necessarily Christian witness.)

More troublesome is the question concerning the witness of a congregation, e. g., a Lutheran congregation, toward other Christians of the neighborhood or area. Sensitiveness to what is considered false doctrine and fear of unionism have often been the rationalization for ordinary apathy — not to say hostility — toward Christians of other groups. Protestants usually approach this problem by joint services as a token of their mutual good will; this is a method obviously inapplicable to Christians who take a confessional position toward the truths of Scripture and it is one which even Protestants sometimes admit does not reach down to the people themselves. It seems to me that the pastor's approach here has to be the same which he employs in training for the calling. Let the Lutheran Christian learn to value the friendship and the Christian conversation of his Presbyterian or Roman Catholic neighbor; and let him learn to speak his own confession of Christ and recommendation of prayer and gratitude for his church and its mutual ministry. Lutherans who are smug and superior but unable to talk about the excellence of their confession and put it to work in their lives of love and concern are not therewith giving a strong witness, but they are breaking the front of Christianity toward the world in that community. Let the pastor feed and lead his Christians to speak the edifying Word of Christ to Christians of whatever stripe or name. Thus the rupture of denominationalism can be bridged without sacrificing the treasure of the truth.

90

In World Outreach

The final facet of parish administration for which we propose to explore the basic theology is world outreach. At first glance we might suppose that this is a contradiction in terms; the parish is the community of Christians organically tied together within the larger community, the neighborhood in which it is located. Hence the parish reaches out into only a tiny sector of the world. Nevertheless we may at once face the situation that denomination and synod bear in on the pastor with appeals and directives in no area of church work more amply and insistently than in missions. In the process the accent is in the nature of the case financial, and we have already discussed the implications of Christian giving for missions. Beyond that detail, is it possible to discuss a theology of pastoral administration with regard to the world outreach of the Christian congregation?

I. The Obligation of the Church to the World

In answering this question we shall indeed grant that we are in part involving earlier implications of our subject rather than entering on new ones. But this subject forces us to clearer insight into the nature of the church itself and thereby clarifies the function of the church's ministry. The church is the gathering of Christians, drawn together not as a statistic, but into a body in which each member has the responsibility of nurturing others. In accomplishing his function the member of the church has basically two tasks. He makes a tragic mistake if he undertakes the one and omits the other; the two fit together like the blades of a shears. The first task of each member of the church as he confronts the world is to keep himself unspotted from the world, for he is set apart from the world for the service of God; his very distinction from the world is essential to this task of displaying God at work in the world. This is the function of being God's holy one, set apart for His service; this is the member of the church as a saint. The other task is to serve the world with the message of life, to live and die for the sake of saving its people one by one. This task, the task of being a servant, is the task of each member. In carrying out these tasks the members of the church are concerned for one another and simultaneously for those outside the church. In carrying out these tasks the members enjoy Christ's gift of pastors and teachers as sustainers and trainers, as helpers toward saintship and servantship.

This is the obligation of the church. We shall be better prepared to confront the pastor's task toward the church if we scrutinize these obligations more closely. The members of the church must keep themselves unspotted from the world. This implies that the world harbors a taint. When we say this we are not talking about the world which is God's creation, the universe which declares the glory of God. But we are talking about the world of human beings which lacks the life and Spirit of God, and which is therefore constantly threatening to bring God's man (who has been drawn out of the world into the fellowship of light) back into the world's orbit. The church is a fellowship in which each member seeks to build the brother with the inner resources of the Spirit of God. But the flesh also seeks for fellowship; it also intercommunicates the counterfeit of life and the will of the devil. In the church, therefore, men remind one another of Christ:

Forasmuch then as Christ hath suffered for us in the flesh, arm yourselves likewise with the same mind; for he that hath suffered in the flesh hath ceased from sin, that he no longer should live the rest of his time in the flesh to the lusts of men but to the will of God. (1 Peter 4:1, 2)

The ministry of the pastor directs Christians to cultivate the life of the Spirit rather than the life of the flesh, in order to set up this distinction from the world which is primary in the Christian witness to the outside; this ministry works by empowering men to empower men.

God hath in due times manifested His word through preaching, which is committed unto me according to the commandment of God our Savior . . . For this cause left I thee [Titus] in

93

Crete, that thou shouldest set in order the things that are wanting, and ordain elders in every city, as I had appointed thee . . . But speak thou the things which become sound doctrine . . . For the grace of God that bringeth salvation hath appeared to all men, teaching us that, denying ungodliness and worldly lusts, we should live soberly, righteously, and godly in this present world . . . these things speak and exhort and rebuke with all authority. . . . Put them in mind to be subject to principalities and powers, to obey magistrates, to be ready to every good work, to speak evil of no man, to be no brawlers, but gentle, shewing all meekness unto all men. (Titus 1:3, 5; 2:1, 11, 12, 15; 3:1, 2)

The climactic test of the holiness of the Christian is his suffering. Here it shows whether or not he is infected by materialism and selfishness, by forgetfulness of the promises of God. It is at this point that the service of the ministry of the church's pastors and teachers is crucial.

The elders which are among you I exhort, who am also an elder and a witness of the sufferings of Christ and also a partaker of the glory that shall be revealed: Feed the flock of God which is among you, taking the oversight thereof not by constraint but willingly, not for filthy lucre but of a ready mind, neither as being lords over God's heritage, but being ensamples to the flock. (1 Peter 5:1-3)

St. Paul addresses one of his most moving reproofs of materialistic concerns expressly to pastors (1 Timothy 6:3-14; note especially 9-12):

. . . They that will be rich fall into temptation and a snare and into many foolish and hurtful lusts which drown men in destruction and perdition. For the love of money is the root of all evil, which while some coveted after, they have erred from the faith, and pierced themselves through with many sorrows. But thou, O man of God, flee these things and follow after righteousness, godliness, faith, love, patience, meekness. Fight the good fight of faith, lay hold on eternal life, whereunto thou art also called and hast professed a good profession before many witnesses.

The other obligation of the church and the church's members, so closely related to the one of being saints and forming the holy Christian church, is the obligation to be servant. The Gentile taint that hangs over the church is to want to rule instead of serve, said the Lord Jesus (Matthew 20:27); and so it remains the mark of Christian people and of the body of Christ that they concern themselves in service, first for one another (Galatians 6:10) and then for all men. This service is concern for the practical needs of men, beginning with their simplest physical necessities and with fellow Christians themselves (1 Timothy 5:8; Matthew 25). But the Christian is a person who has insight into the fact that the real and everlasting life is the life in God's dimension, and that therefore his service must ultimately convey this everlasting sort of life; the great directive is First John and its thrust to love men as God first loved us in Christ. This means that the absorbing service and ministry of God's people to their world is to make disciples of them; that is the great commission (Matthew 28:19). A disciple is not simply a saved person or one immunized against hell fire; but he is a learner, one brought into a listening and nurturing relationship with Jesus Christ Himself by others who are in that same relationship.

The New Testament reveals a close affinity between the business of being a saint and being a servant. Thus St. Peter exhorts to the kind of citizenship that stops the evil gossip about Christians and starts them asking the right questions about their faith and hope:

> . . . Abstain from fleshly lusts, which war against the soul, having your conversation honest among the Gentiles, that, whereas they speak against you as evildoers, they may by your good works, which they shall behold, glorify God in the day of visitation . . . For so is the will of God, that with well doing ye may put to silence the ignorance of foolish men, as free, and not using your liberty for a cloke of maliciousness, but as the servants of God. (1 Peter 2:11, 12, 15, 16)

St. Paul shows that the structure of government has as its purpose the unimpeded functioning of the Christian's message of the Gospel to the surrounding world (1 Timothy 2:1-8). He himself functions as a pastoral administrator in his counsel to Timothy and the teachers at work under Timothy that they move their people to pray for this sort of government, and that Christian men and women behave themselves in agreement with this message. (Vv. 9-15)

96

True, much of this service, put to work particularly in the callings to Christians, exerts itself in community witness. But the point of our consideration today is that as Christians learn to understand the nature of their world and the nature of their church, their outreach can not possibly halt at any one barrier of attitude or space. More exactly, as they find themselves hampered by fleshly attitudes impeding the outreach, their fellow Christians and their pastors and teachers are to be the people who help them to overcome and to bring the church into action toward the world whereever they may be.

The simplest obstacle is prejudice. Ephesians is a great instance of pastoral concern regarding barriers blocking edification between Jewish Christians and Gentile Christians in the same community. St. Paul links the removal of this barrier to his basic assignment to preach the Gospel; for as he succeeds in building the body of Christ in the place, he holds up before the world the power of Christ and His Gospel.

> Unto me, who am less than the least of all saints, is this grace given, that I should preach among the Gentiles the unsearchable riches of Christ and to make all men see what is the fellowship of the mystery, which from the beginning of the world hath been hid in God, who created all things by Jesus Christ, to the intent that now unto the principalities and powers in heavenly places might be known by the church the manifold wisdom of God. (Ephesians 3:8-10)

The parallel obstacle is dissension. Philippians is a case study of the apostle seeking to apply the Gos-

97

pel to a Christian congregation and to its mutual provision of it in its midst, so that the outreach to the world might not be impeded by internal bickering.

Do all things without murmurings and disputings that ye may be blameless and harmless, the sons of God, without rebuke, in the midst of a crooked and perverse nation, among whom ye shine as lights in the world: holding forth the word of life; that I may rejoice in the day of Christ that I have not run in vain neither laboured in vain. (Philippians 2:14-16)

The basic attitude in Christians toward one another and for their world outreach has to be the will to serve. That means to regard the next man as the person for whom the Christian lives, whether that next man be in his own family or his next door neighbor or the fellow workman or the fellow parishioner, or whether it be a man of another color and language on the other side of the globe. And the basic task of the pastor as feeder and leader is to impart the Gospel through which Christian fellowship is initiated and conserved, and to oversee the tasks of people bringing this Gospel to bear upon one another and serving men wherever they can reach them.

II. The Pastor's Administration of the Parish in World Outreach

Let us observe some of the operations in this direction and oversight of the parish.

The first is obviously to hold up before the parish the directive of the great commission. This can become so trite and be said in such unpleasant language —

give money to help the heathen, keep up the budget contributions to the denomination — that it appears valueless. This can be said as though the power for carrying it out lies in the pressure of the pastor and his organization; this happens when the pastor tries to lead without feeding. The food for the task is that people are confronted with the redeeming act of Jesus Christ by which they are placed in His service; they see the love of Christ for them by which they are constrained to do His work; and His greatest work is that men are made and kept His disciples.

But the great commission isn't stay and pay, but go and disciple. Even the staying and paying becomes a superstitious and disruptive act of Christians unless they realize that their giving for missions is a part of their own going and that the missionary enterprise which their money staffs and promotes is simply the labor of members of the body of Christ of which all the others are members too. Hence training for making disciples and enrolling in the mission effort means enlisting in a total effort. This does not complicate but rather simplifies the task. For the task is that people be reached with the Gospel, and be reached throughout the world. This goal can be said in ways that are too optimistic and unrealistic — "evangelize the world in this generation" — so that Christians think the pastor is recommending something that can't be done anyway, and therefore rest with their own efforts listless and symbolical rather than actual. But this goal can be set forth too partially and thus the leading of the pastor becomes hampered.

It is easy to hide behind Luther's classic dictum

that the church proceeds through the world like a thundershower; it moves of itself, and the individual does little for or against it. Usually this hampering of the mission objective occurs when a pastor or parish says: We first have to take care of our own community. When we are established and have our debts paid and have really reached every person in our area, then it will be reasonable to help with the worldwide effort. This must be wrong *eo ipso,* for if it could ever be true, then all would be heathen and the Gospel would never have penetrated to our land and generation, and the first Christians would still be busy in Palestine.

The church's program of mission outreach is simply the functioning of the body of Christ by which the member of the church in one place is able to thrust the Gospel into people wherever else Christ's body is at work. Hence it should be logically and theologically impossible for a man to preach toward fund raising for missions and not toward the Christian witness of his hearers to their own community; and vice versa. It should be impossible to say: If we cannot go, we can pay; or, if we cannot go and cannot pay, we can at least pray. If we are Christians, we are going; we are moving the frontier of the Christian church out over our own children at our table, and over the neighbor next door and over the fellow member of our parish and his children; and we are going throughout the world by means of our own voice and hand and by means of voices and hands with which we are membered and united. Anything short of that is dismemberment of the holy Christian church, the body of Christ.

100

To make this work, the pastor must not merely show the logic of the working of the body of Christ, but he has to preach and teach the headship of Christ, who works in the body and imparts His drive of love to the individual members of the body. This dynamic of the Gospel applied to the Christian right in the home parish can fructify the entire significance of a synodical mission program. A synod is only an advisory body, we sometimes say, as we chafe under mission allotments and programs. This is a half-truth. What's true about it is that no Christian has the right to work toward any other Christian with anything more than advice — if by that we mean the mutual stimulation of remembering the high-priestly work of Jesus Christ and His intercession at this moment for us before the throne of the grace of God. What's wrong about it is that if the work of the church and the people of the church are Christian we are very much the body of Christ and our work with and for each other has to be recognized in those terms and not just in the semisecular ones of fund raising or national administration.

This sense of teamwork in the body of Christ should animate our thinking about what we do as representatives of the church, its members at work at that moment — wherever we are. We spoke much of this in connection with Christian witness in the community. It pertains to the worldwide task. The Christian in East Germany should think of us as missionaries to the capitalistic United States. The Christian in Mexico should think of the Canadian Christian as his worker in Canada. We think of Christian missionaries throughout the world as our fellow workmen in their posts; but they should think of us as their fellow workmen in our area. Our thought of one another is to be the thought of love, the desire to sustain and uphold one another in Christ through the remembrance of His redeeming work. The father is missionary of the church to the people whom he meets in his calling, and the family prays with and for him as he fares forth and feeds him with the Gospel as well as breakfast food at the start of the day. And the pastor sees to it that this food is shared.

But simultaneously we who are missionaries (whether at home or abroad depends on our stance at the moment) have to be helped to love those to whom we bring the Gospel and challenge to be disciples. Synonym of disciple is servant. Throughout the world non-Christian people are to see Christians as gentle folk, growing in the understanding of their own Savior, concerned for the simple welfare of the people whom they reach and with whom they live, and anxious that their neighbors should know more of Him whom they are learning more intimately day by day: Jesus Christ. We feel embarrassed at the idea of the materialistic and blatant American who becomes the image of our fellow citizen in a foreign land. He's ugly because he's self-assured, well-fed, ready to pluck personal and commercial advantage from others wherever he meets them, convinced of his own superiority, loud, and intolerant. The picture that the New Testament gives of the Christian in a community of non-Christians — or among Christians, for that matter — is that he is quiet, anxious to serve and improve the other person, confident of the helpful and saving truth of Jesus Christ and concerned somehow and by every means to share it with others; he does not pose as an authority in religion but as a seeker for God who is finding Him through Jesus Christ; he does not pose as superior to other people but is anxious to put them on his track of learning. To be people of this order Christians have to be fed continually by the message of Christ, who Himself became every man's servant and said, "Learn of Me, for I am meek and lowly in heart." The pastor is the person who is responsible for feeding and implementing the feeding with this food.

Again the worldwide nature of the body of Christ becomes apparent. We see why Jesus Christ was so concerned (frequently by stressing the interracial accent of his objective as in the parable of the Good Samaritan) that His followers might love all without respect of persons or partiality. Several of us asked Dr. Edwin T. Dahlberg, then president of the National Council of Churches of Christ in the United States, how he envisioned the message of a worldwide Gospel taking hold at the grass roots of the local congregation. He answered: "My son is a medical missionary in Burma, a few miles from the communist border. When an anti-integration incident occurs in St. Louis, the story appears in their daily paper the next morning." The New Testament gives us two briefings for disciples of Christ on the front of witnessing to people. The one is in the words of the Lord Jesus, Matthew 5–7; the other is the First Epistle of Peter. Both set forth the agonizingly high ideal of the Christian

103

throughout the world: loving people who have no claim on him and only that they might learn to glorify the Father. This ideal cannot be met unless as Christians we first are overcome by Christ Jesus and His love toward us. The pastor feeds with that love and leads people to prove it.

As the tides of nationalism rise higher and the antipathy for Western culture grows deeper, a Western church body becomes more and more dependent on nonprofessional missionaries; we realized earlier in this study that parish administration is simply implementing as many ministries in a local congregation as there are people, and not complete dependence on the services of professionals. We try to train professionals before we send them into the parishes and missions of the world. The pastor and local parish are in the business of training nonprofessionals as they go into their callings throughout the world. Every visitor to Hawaii has been amazed at the multiracial and yet compact and busy church life of a congregation like Our Redeemer Lutheran Church. The pastor and his family and the teachers of the parish school functioned well in the picture. But amazing was the manner in which Christian business men and women thousands of miles from the Midwestern churches and schools in which they had been reared fitted themselves into this new situation and made their contribution to edification. They were as genuinely missionaries on the front of the world outreach as were the professionals.

Many congregations are returning to a practice which has always been the method of many Protestant denominations, that is, to regard certain missionary workers on foreign fields as specifically their concern, paid for from the congregational budget and remembered in specific prayers of the church. This method is especially helpful in the process of parish administration of world missions. Also where it does not take this form, pastor and people should arrive at a sense of personal concern for the church's missionaries and newfound lay believers in all the world. The recent practice of supplying the church with names and addresses of missionary workers at Christmastime is useful for stimulating at least token concern. This can be multiplied in many ways on the level of adults and children. Motion pictures on medical missions, such as *A Place to Go*, supplied by the Wheat Ridge Foundation (Chicago, Illinois), are powerful promotion for genuine concern for Christians in need throughout the world; the foundation itself is a worthy link in the church's mission program implementing this love.

III. The Pastor's Concern for the Pastor

Much of our discussion in the previous pages may seem to have been on an idealistic level. It read well and sounded good but the performance seems quite improbable. This is due in part to the fact that we are summarizing and that the actual cases have to be worked out in practice. It is also due to the fact that this side of the grave the Christian life is not perfect. Any guidance Christians give one another toward richer life in Christ is always hampered by obstacles. The lust of the flesh, the lust of the eyes, and the pride of life seek to blind the eyes of Christian pilgrims at every turn of the way. This is why we talk of pastors and teachers as feeders and leaders. They are not engineers of toy trains who simply throw the switches and let the trains run their course. But they are gardeners who are raising a crop that matures slowly and is hampered all the way by weeds and drought and pests.

We fail to make one of our most necessary contributions if we omit a word to pastors and teachers about nurturing themselves. "The husbandman must first be partaker of the fruits," St. Paul tells Timothy. The fruit of the pastor's work is that his man comes to faith and is sustained in faith. But the sharecropper for God who is raising that fruit needs some himself. Illustrations about shepherds and flocks, or farmers and crops, break down at this point. The shepherd is also a sheep. The farmer is also grain in the field. He needs feeding and leading as much as do the people who are his clients and charges. He needs cultivation along with every branch on the one Vine, which is Jesus Christ.

We might take time to discuss some of the formal methods of safeguarding this nurture of the pastor so that he continues to do a good job of feeding and leading. These would involve processes of personal devotion and nurture, like the use of John Doberstein's *Minister's Prayer Book,* the employing of a father confessor for regular confession and absolution, the fructifying of gatherings of professionals in conferences and study groups, the enhancing of professional skills through graduate study and reading. I do not wish to belittle any of these by this brief reference. But

I want to stress our picture of the pastor as shepherd and husbandman, and the fact that he must be thought of also as a member of the flock. He is a member of the body of Christ, and as such the hand that sometimes prods and massages other portions of the body into activity. But that does not mean that the rest of the body does not do something for him too.

As the pastor and teacher administrates his parish he holds before it many goals of spiritual life; he awakens and puts to use many gifts of the Holy Spirit for the edification of all. At this point we must remind ourselves that one of these goals is the spiritual care also of the pastor and teacher and all professionals and semiprofessionals of the congregation. Spiritual gifts are to be discerned and used also for nurture of the pastor. Noteworthy are the epistles with their constant stress on the care that congregations owe their spiritual teachers and leaders. The people are to share every good thing with them (Galatians 6:6) and to deem them worthy of suitable compensation (1 Timothy 5:17). They are to recognize and fit themselves into the program of nurture toward God which they operate (Hebrews 13:9, 17). St. Paul rejoiced not merely in the fact that he had been able to speak the Gospel to the people to whom he wrote, but that he had shared the Gospel with them, which means *that he had listened to them speaking it to him* as well:

I thank my God upon every remembrance of you, always in every prayer of mine for you all making request with joy, for your fellowship in the Gospel from the first day until now, being confident of this very thing that He which hath begun a good work in you will perform it until the day of Jesus Christ; even as it is meet for me to think this of you all, because I have you in my heart; inasmuch as both in my bonds and in the defence and confirmation of the Gospel, ye are all partakers of my grace. (Philippians 1:3-7)

As the pastor administrates the parish, then, and initiates chain reactions triggered by the Gospel, he himself is again and again to become a target of that program. This begins in his worship with his people: he speaks not so much to his people as with them, and they are speaking the same message to him that he has for them; he is not so much preaching to himself as saying that which the people are preaching to him. Here it is of especial importance, it seems to me, that the pastor should be receiving Holy Communion with his people; thus they preach the Lord's death to him as he has preached it to them. And the church organist should not be exempt from Holy Communion because there is nobody to relieve him during the distribution; let the people sit in decorous silence or sing without accompaniment as the organist takes his place before the altar with the people.

Many pastors find it difficult to feed themselves with the Word which they feed to others. The skill of communicating seems to be output instead of intake. Men must therefore discover that communication, in the exact sense, always includes feedback, intake from the person communicated to; in Paul's phrase, we are in a "fellowship," a mutual sharing, of the Gospel every time we speak it to a Christian. This is why

Eduard Thurneysen can say of the pastor's care of his sick and perplexed, "Die Seelsorge ist ein Gespräch," pastoral care is two-way conversation. This is why St. Paul can tell Timothy (1 Timothy 4:16) that when he keeps on teaching his hearers he saves not only them but also himself; for he then listens to their word as well as to his own as the power of God unto salvation. When the pastor therefore applies the Gospel of God as motivation not merely to the primary listener, but to the people whom he is deploying to speak that saving word to others — that is administration — he is himself caught up in the nurture of the church and the body of Christ in that place as it grows up in Christ in all things.

Of peak importance in the process of parish administration is the mutual nurture with the Gospel of God of the men and women who work with the pastor in the administrative task: the teachers and board people in Christian education, the elders and trustees and voting members in the overall structure of parish business, the finance committees and officials in the program of Christian giving. This mutual nurture has to be a good deal more than the opening or closing of a meeting with prayer. It must indeed be the turning of the hearts of the participants to God in prayer — especially in the crises of difficulty or perplexity concerning deficiencies in parish nurture, disasters or impasses in program, or delinquencies of members. But always there must be mutual nurture through contemplation of the Lord of the Church, of the sacrifice by which He made us His, of the intercession by which He keeps us at our tasks — the message which is at once food to eat and food to distribute. As the leader of the parish shares in such moments of feeding, he is himself empowered for the leading.

This constant feeding *by* the feeder is crucial; thus we can conclude where we began with a thought for the overworked parish administrator and the erosion of his own spiritual life by tasks which have become secular rather than pastoral. He need not withdraw himself into the remote fastnesses of the contemplative life; he can stay with his people at their tasks. But let him feed the people with the bread of life, the atonement of our Lord and its message in words and in the sacraments. And let him eat that bread. ". . . We will give ourselves continually to prayer, and to the ministry of the Word," said the apostles in that notable document about parish administration, the choosing of the helpers in Jerusalem (Acts 6:1-7). The division of duties was good administration. That the helpers were men of honest report, full of the Holy Ghost and wisdom, was good personnel management for the church. But as the apostles now concentrated on the administration of the services of the church and the preaching of the Gospel, we can be sure that they listened as well as spoke. For we are told that "the Word of God increased." Thus, when the pastor feeds and leads, let him be fed and led, that through him and around him the Word of God may reach its mark and God's plan be achieved to rescue men from the kingdom of Satan and transplant them in the kingdom of His Son.

Bibliography

(This list of readings is supplied at the request of some of the members of the Parish Administration Institute of 1960)

The writer's position is expressed in print in Chapter i of *The Pastor at Work* (St. Louis: Concordia Publishing House, 1960); Chapters ii, ix, xxx, xliii–xlv of *Preaching for the Church* (St. Louis: Concordia, 1959); "The Practice of Holy Communion," *The Abiding Word*, III (St. Louis: Concordia, 1960), 531 ff.; "The Body of Christ," *Proceedings of the Atlantic District* (1958); "The Spiritual Life of the Teacher," *Lutheran Education*, XCV, 2 (October 1959), 56 ff.; "The Universal Priesthood and the Pastor," *Concordia Theological Monthly*, XIX, 8 (August 1948), 561 ff. "Kerygma and Didache in Christian Education" ibid. XXXII, 4 (April 1961), 197 ff.

Useful monographs on the church and the interaction of church members are Dietrich Bonhoeffer, *Life Together*, trans. John W. Doberstein (New York: Harper & Sons, 1954); Suzanne de Dietrich, *The Witnessing Community* (Philadelphia: Westminster Press, 1958); Daniel Jenkins, *The Strangeness of the Church* (Garden City, N. Y.: Doubleday and Company, Inc., 1955); Hendrik Kraemer, *The Communication of the Christian Faith* (Philadelphia: Westminster, 1956); Paul S. Minear, *Horizons of Christian Community* (St. Louis: Bethany Press, 1959); D. T. Niles, *The Preacher's Task and the Stone of Stumbling* (New York: Harper, 1958).

On the work of the pastor note H. Grady Davis, "The Ministry in the New Testament," *Chicago Lutheran Seminary Record*, LVII, 3 (July 1952); H. Richard Niebuhr, *The Purpose of the Church and Its Ministry* (New York: Harper, 1956); Robert N. Rodenmayer, *We Have This Ministry* (New York: Harper, 1959). On the spiritual life of the pastor see *Minister's Prayer Book*, ed. John W. Doberstein (Philadelphia: Muhlenberg Press, 1959); Gustav Jensen, *The Ministry*, trans. O. E. Brandt (Minneapolis: Augsburg Publishing House, 1958); Daniel T. Niles, *The Preacher's Calling to Be Servant* (New York: Harper, 1959); Daniel Day Williams, *The Minister and the Care of Souls* (New York: Harper, 1961); Eduard Thurneysen, *A Theology of Pastoral Care* (Richmond: John Knox Press, 1961).

On the pastorate at work in the mutual operations of the parish note Tom Allan, *The Face of My Parish* (New York: Harper, 1957); Paul Rowntree Clifford, *The Mission of the Local Church* (London: SCM Press, 1953).